Memorialized Records of Lexington District, South Carolina

1814-1825

Brent H. Holcomb

HERITAGE BOOKS
2016

HERITAGE BOOKS
AN IMPRINT OF HERITAGE BOOKS, INC.

Books, CDs, and more—Worldwide

For our listing of thousands of titles see our website
at
www.HeritageBooks.com

Published 2016 by
HERITAGE BOOKS, INC.
Publishing Division
5810 Ruatan Street
Berwyn Heights, Md. 20740

Copyright © 1978 by The Rev. Silas Emmett Lucas, Jr.

Copyright © assigned to Brent H. Holcomb 1989

*Our thanks to Mr. J. R. Fennell, Jr., Director of the Lexington County Museum,
for the image of the Lexington District Clerk of Court Seal
and permission to use it in this publication.*

All rights reserved. No part of this book may be reproduced or transmitted in any form or by any means, electronic or mechanical, including photocopying, recording or by any information storage and retrieval system without written permission from the author, except for the inclusion of brief quotations in a review.

International Standard Book Numbers
Paperbound: 978-0-7884-5738-8
Clothbound: 978-0-7884-5975-7

INTRODUCTION

Since the first publication of this volume in 1977 there has been a tremendous increase in interest in early Lexington County genealogy. A genealogical association has been formed in Lexington County and has been successful in locating some original deeds and copies of other records. Genealogical research in Lexington County/District has been a problem because of the major record losses. The deeds prior to 1839 and the probate records prior to 1865 were destroyed by fire in 1865. Fortunately the deeds beginning with Book M (1839) have survived. By the county court act of 1785, the clerk of each county was supposed to send in a list of probates and deeds for each year to the Secretary of State. These lists are generally known as the memorialized records, but they should not be confused with the colonial series of Land Memorials. The extent to which the clerks complied with the act is unknown, as only a few of these lists are extant. A few of these records were known to exist for Lexington District, but the bulk of them were discovered among the legislative papers in 1976 and were brought to my attention by Mr. Horace Fraser Rudisill of Darlington, South Carolina. These lists cover the year 1814-1825, but the lists of deeds contain many instruments executed much earlier, some prior to the Revolution. The original lists are available at the South Carolina Archives and can be consulted there. These lists are published here verbatim or as nearly so as possible. Some years apparently have two sets of memorialized deeds. The reason for this duplication is not known. The actual deed books and the wills and administrations have not survived.

A few hints may be helpful in using these memorialized records: the entries from the Comr in Equity C D or N D are deeds from the Court of Equity for Columbia District (Lexington, Richland, and Fairfield) or for Newberry District. These equity files are extant at the South Carolina Archives. The fork between the Broad and Saluda Rivers (sometimes abbreviated f B & S) is synonymous with the Dutch Fork, so called because of the large German (Deutsch) population which settled there. Sometimes more information on the parties mentioned in these deeds can be found by checking a subsequent deed for the property, wherein the grantee of the memorialized deed is the grantor of a deed recorded after 1839. Usually a long chain of title, or derivation clause, is recited.

Brent H. Holcomb
January 5, 1989

"Dead Poll for Lexi

Names of Deceased	Names of Executors	Names of Administrators
Gregory Dorathy	Nuncupative Will	admr with the will anne Baruch Snelgrove
Baugh Leonard John	John Baugh & Abram Geiger	
Kaigler John		Margaret & Andrew Kaig]
Minick George B	Wm Summer) who & John Counts) refused to Qualify	Wm Minick annexed with the will
Boozer Jacob		Boozer Jacob
Koon John Henry		Jacob & Samuel Koon
Arthur Ambrose		Elisha Daniel
Hamiter Michael		George Aull
Smith Thomas	Catherine & Thos Smith	
Gartman Philip	Frederick Kelly	
Geiger John	Wm Geiger & Saml Kennerly	
Siebles Jacob		Sarah & Henry Siebles

John McCreless, Ordinary

District in the year 1815."

Penalty of Bond	Time of Qualification
$600	17th January 1815
	27 January 1815
$11,000	26 Jan ditto
$500	12 March ditto
$2,000	10th March ditto
$4,000	22d April ditto
$100	20th March ditto
$1,000	9th October ditto
	23 ditto ditto
	5th December ditto
	13th November Do
$14,000	27th November Do

"Dead Roll for Lexington District in

Names of Deceased	Names of Executors	Names of administra
Mathias Coogler		John & George Coogle
Dublin a free black man		Jesse Arthur
Maria Rea		James Rives & James
Thomas B. Leonard		John Leonard Cayce
William Snelgrove	Thomas K. Poindexter) & Godfrey Harman)	
John Lowerman		William C. Lowerman
Martin Hidle		John Hidle
Thomas Burket		Margaret Burket &) John Ouattlebom)
George Setzler		John Setzler
Hargrove Arthur	Mary Arthur, R. Pearce, J. R. Arthur, Henry Arthur	
Christian Rister		John Adam Rister
John Geiger	Harman & Wm Geiger	
Frederick Wise		Mary Wise
Christian Lightner		Abigail Lightner
Margaret Zimmerly	John Nichols	
Michael Oswalt		Catharine Oswalt
Samuel Drafts	West Caughman, Daniel &) Jacob Drafts)	
Laurence Rambo		Daniel Rambo
Jacob Boozer		Jacob Drafts & David Boozer
Thomas Bartlet		Rhody Bartlett & Henry Miller

"South Carolina Lexington District

  I John McCreless ordinary for the District afores do hereby certify that the within is a correct and tr account of the Wills Proved, and the administrations granted by me for the year Ending the last day of December 1817.

      John McCreless ordinary "

year Ending the last of December 1817."

Names of the Securities	Penalty of Bonds	Time of Qualification	
John Metz & John Weed	$300	20th February	1817
Elisha Daniel & John Arthur	$500	12th March	Do
James Pous	$2000	4th March	Do
John Thomas & John Grim	$8000	19th April	Do
		Will proved 24th April 1817	
John Craps & Wm Slagle	$3000	23rd day of May	Do
N. Hane & H Muller	$9000	24th June	Do
John W. Lee	$8000	30th June	Do
John Countz & Wm. F Houseal	$400	25th August	Do
		Will proved 30th August 1817	
James daily & Jesse W. Rhaw	$5,000	6th October	Do
		8th Do	Do
West Caughman & Michael Craps	$500	7th Do	Do
Davis Austin & John Caughman	$1,000	15th Do	Do
		Will proved 3rd November 1817	
Micajah Martin & Henry Oswalt	$1,000	6th Do Do	
		Will proved 20th November 1817	
Amos Banks	$1,000	1st December	Do
West Caughman & Emanl Corley	$8000	20th Do	Do
Leonard Baugh	$800	30th Do	Do

"Dead Poll for Lexington

Names of Deceased	Names of Executors	Names of Administrators
Benedict Mayer	Margt. Mayer John Adam Mayer	
William Butler		Elizabeth Butler
Charles F. Conheim	Martha Conheim Jacob Huffman	
Jane Elison		Samuel Corbin
Michael Hite		Christian Hite
Philip Hohaimer		Thomas Sheppard
John Minick Junr.		Michael Barr
Thomas Derick		Jacob Derick
Peter Effler		Catharine Effler
Gasper Souter	John Souter, Jacob Souter	
Nancy Bickley		John Bickley
Simeon Eleazar	Henry Eleazer	
Michael Eragle		Uriah Wessinger Isaac Lybrand
Jonas Mathias		Sarah Mathias, John Mathias
Peter Wissenhunt		William Wissenhunt
Mary Summer	Benedict Mayer, Henry Ruff) Margt. Houseal, Geo. Eigleberger)	
Andrew Kaigler		John Drehr, Thomas Shular
Henry Summer		John Countz (Carpenter)
James Callaham		Benjamin Jefcoat
William Summer		John Summer

"A true Extract from the Records for the year 1818"
John McCreless O. L. D.

District For the year 1818."

Names of Securities	Amount of Bonds	Time of Qualification
		8th January 1818
John Thomas, John Haugabook	$20,000	9th do do
		16th March do
John Cates, Joseph Cryder	$2,000	13th do do
Wm Lybrand, Michael Eragle	$500	10 do do
John Bouknight, John Bouknight Jr.	$400	20th April do
John C. Bell, Amos Banks	$8,000	10th do do
George Lorick, John Derick	$4000	20th do do
John Friday, James Cayce	$500	9th June do
		11th July do
Jacob Bick, Samuel Wessinger Junr.	$8,000	13th do do
		3d August do
John Lybrand, Uriah Bickley	$4000	3d do do
Matthias Senn John Matthias	$2,000	10th do do
William Geiger, John Averhart	$3,000	17th do do
		18th Septr do
Samuel Koon John Shular	$10,000	2d October 1818
George Eigleberger, John Counts	$10,000	13th do do
David Callaham, John Baughman	$2,000	19th do do
George Aull, Henry Kunkle	$5,000	10th Novr do

"Dead Roll for Lexington

Names of Deceased	Names of Executors	Names of Administrators
James Brown		Thomas Quiter
John Countz		Samuel Buzby
Jacob Nicholas		Mary Nicholas widow
Mathias Wingert		Samuel Archer
Dr. Luke Cheesbrough		Jona L. Chessbrough
George Derick		John H. Derick &) Andrew Derick)
Revd. Jno H. Winkhouse	Harmond Sullan & Catharine Elizabeth Winkhouse)	
John Mathias	Sebastian Younginger &) Jacob Huffman)	
Catharine Bugh	John Shuler &) John Kleckley)	
Samuel Koon	Thomas Rives &) Thomas Burket)	
Adam Setzler	Capt John Epting) John Setzler)	
Mary Minick		Michael Barr
Jesse Geiger		William J. Geiger
John Kleckley		Thomas Shuler
Brinkly Vick		Mary Vick (widow)
William Geiger		Nancy Geiger (widow)
David Autrey		Henry Eleazer
John Jones		Wes Coughman
Peter Coogle		David Coogle will annexed Daniel Meze

Agreeable to the Act of the General Assembly Passed 1789 I herewith Transmit the above Dead Roll to the office of Secretary of State for Lexington District for the year ending January 1821.

January 15th 1821   Arthur H. Fort   Ordinary L D

District in the year 1820."

Names of the Securities	Penalty of Bonds	Time of Qualification
John Rodwitz(?)	$100	21st June 1820
Michael Stuck	100	10 June 1820
George Leaphart) Thomas Burket)	500	8 Septr 1820
George Gross	500	11th Septr 1820
John Thomas	1,000	30 Augt 1820
John Derick) Jacob Bickly)	4,000	23 Octo 1820
		June the 9th 1820
		Nov 23 1820
		" 15 1820 John Shuler one only qualified
		Qualified Thomas Rives only 7th Decr 1820
		26th do 1820
John M(?) Lee) John Shealy)	2,000	9th October 1820
Amos Banks	300	25th September 1820
John Awengard) Jacob Kleckley)	2000	18th Nov 1820
Henry Oswalt & George Oswalt		17th do 1820
Henry Muller) Godfrey Kirsh)	$6000	22d December 1820
George Lindler &) John A Rister)	700	22rd do 1820
John Meetze &) Amos Banks)	$400	29th do 1820
Jacob Kleckley John Coogle	200	26th December 1820

"Dead Roll in Lexington District

Names of Deceased	Names of Executor	Names of Administrators
Lewis Friday		John Swygert
Mary Agnes Sonn		Andrew Son (deed annexed)
Lew Ellen Threwits		John Thomas
James Rogers		George Crapps
James Smith		Daniel Bouknight
Jacob Pickley		Samuel Pickley
Sibbelly Snider		Christian Freshly (Will and.)
John Friday		Emanuel Friday & John Brice
Barnet Lybrand	Wills West Coughman &) Jacob Kelly)	
Henry Gallman	Reuben E. Slappy) William H Lee)	
Jacob Epting	George Epting	
John Wolfe	Lewis Pou & Jacob Wolfe	
Elizabeth Berry		Jacob Honold and. will

The above is a memorial of administrations and Probates Granted for the District of Lexington in the year of our Lord one thousand eight hundred twenty one

        A H Fort ordy L D

Returned to Secretary for the Year of 1821."

Securities names	Penal[ty] of Bond	Time of Qualification
Christian Swygert) Amos Banks)	$550.00	13th January 1821
Abraham Fulmer) Christian Swygert)	2000.00	5th February 1821
David Boozer	500	7 Do Do
John Crapps &) David Jumper)	2500.00	22nd May Do
Andrew Derick	250.00	8th March Do
Baruch Snelgrove) Joseph Pickly)	1000.00	27th October Do
George Meetze) John Boughnight Jr.)	1000.00	31st Do Do
William Kinsler) Lewis Pou)	2000.00	13th November Do
		March 21st 1821
		20th Septr Do
		30th Octr Do
		3rd January 1822
William See & Jacob Rice	$50	12th Do Do

"Memorial of Probates of Wills & Administrations
Thousand eight Hundred and twenty two certified by

Names of Decd.	Executors	Administrators
George Lowerman omitted in last return		Ann Katharine Lowerman John Lowerman
Godfrey Airhart		John Airhart & Martin Lybrand
William Taylor (Sandy Run)	will annexed	William P. Taylor
Eliza Boozer		William See
Adam Black		John Black
Mrs. Barbara Gartman		Jacob Rall
Mrs. Katharine Keizler		Jacob Keizler
John Haugabook		Levi Haugabook
George Shirey	will annexed	Martin Free
William Baker		Catharine Baker
George Taylor		John Taylor
John Stingely		Sarah Stingley &) Geo Stingley)
Asel Roberts		Absalom Roberts) Jno Coughman
George Kelly		Jacob Kelly
George Haltiwanger		H F Haltiwanger
John Sawyer	will annexed	Geo Sawyer & A W Shealy
John H Eiffert		Mary Eiffert) Wm C Mitchel)
Mark Seas	William Summer) Fredk Seas)	
Zachariah Unger	Mary Unger) Jacob Lowerman)	

Granted in Lexington District in the Year of Our Lord one
A H Fort Ordinary for said District."

Penal[ty] of Bond	Sureties	Time Qualified
$6000	Jacob Pickly &) Henry Lybrand)	10th Feby 1821
400	Jno Meetze & Jno Swygert	14th January do*
5000	Lavinia Taylor, Moses Henton	15th March do
400	Jacob Luts & David Hendriz	4th March do
600	David Risinger & D Lomanick	5th Apl do
400	Wm Derit & Emanuel Corley	25th March do
500	Geo Keizler, Fredk Rall	9th Apl do
2000	West Coughman & M Hook	3rd June do
100	George Mayer & Jacob Mayer	31st May do
300	Christian Rall & John Withers	14th July do
100	Martin Fikes & John Fikes	3rd Augt do
1500	Godfrey Stingley) Jacob Harmon)	13th Septr do
1000	West Coughman) John Meetze)	20th Nov do
300	Saml Kelly & Barbara Corly	29 do do
1200	Geo Lindler & J A Rister	" " "
3000	M. Barr & A. Banks	19th Octr do
5000	Forest Mitchel) Sion Mitchel)	2nd Decr do
		21st Augt do
		13 do do

*This probably should read 1822, and only the first entry is 1821.

"Memmorial of Probates of Wills and administrations in eight Hundred and twenty three and twenty four Transmitted A. H. Fort ordinary for said District February 1825."

Names Decd.	Executors	Administrators
Jonathan Gilbert		Nancy Gilbert
Alexr B Stark		Sarah Stark
James H. Jenkins		Thos K. Poindexter
Jacob Rice		John S. Addy
David Metz		George Metz
Godfrey Stingeley		Jacob Harmon &) Jacob Stingeley)
John P. Bond		Henry H. Hill & Stephen Daniel
Agnes Son		Andrew Son
Frederick Bough		Michael Wessinger
Henry F. Minick		Jacob Minick
John See		John W. Seay
Davis Austen		Catharine Austin &) John Rall)
Samuel Kennerly		Elizabeth Kennerly &) Thomas K. Poindexter)
Zachariah Unger	Mary Unger &) Jacob Lowerman)	
Samuel Corbin	Wm. P. Corben	
William Arthur	Daniel Morgan	
Jacob Chapp	Wm Kinsler	
Margaret Slappy	A Geiger & Jacob Bell	
Adam Countz	Jacob Swygert	

Lexington District in the years of our Lord one Thousand
to the Secretarys of States office certified by

Penal[ty] of Bond	Securities Names	Time of Qualification		
$1000	Daniel Lightner & James Calk	January	20th	1823
$20,000	Thomas Lemar, Robert Warring & Thos Rall	March	20th	do
100	G. Haltiwanger & John Gable	May	23rd	do
10,000	John W Lee & John Black	Nov.	10th	do
2000	Joseph Metz & Peter Metz	Decr.	12th	do
2000	Andrew Derick & George Stingley	"	29	do
40,000	William Daniel, Jeremiah Hatcher,) Theos. Hill, Elijah Watson &) John Bales (Bates?)	Octr.	1st	do
2000	Jacob Countz & Adam Mayer	Nov.	11th	do
500	John D. Sharp & John Ruff	Decr.	19th	do
600	Uriah Mayer & George Lindler	Apl	26th	1824
2000	Christian Rall & Wm Taylor	August	12th	do
60,000	Jacob Rall, Fred'k Rall,) Deril Harrison & Absalom Roberts)	"	12th	do
16,000	Thomas Rall, James Kennerly &) Drury Davis)	Octr.	26th	do
		Augt	13th	1822
		January	14th	1823
		do	8	1824
		July	27th	do
		Feby	15th	do
		Nov	19th	do

"A List of Probates and Administrations had in
Thousand Eight Hundred and twenty five certified

Names of Decd	Executors names	Administrators Names
James Y. Smith		Eleanor Smith &) Jno McCreless)
William Stagner		Absalom Hendrix
William Livingston		Barnet Livingston
J. J. Swygert		Michael Louck
Jacob Boozer		David Boozer
Nancy Metz		Jacob Metz
Conrod Slice		Uriah Slice
Doctor H. F. Schmitz	Maria Schmitz &) Adam Schmitz)	
Barnet Hoyler	Daniel Hoyler &) Gabriel Hoyler)	
George Slappy	Jacob C. Slappy	
John Rice	David Kyzer	

Lexington District in the year of our Lord one by A H Fort Ordinary of said District."

Penalty of Bonds	Securities Names	Date of Probate or Admn.
$500.00	Amos Banks & Alexander Stewart	27th June 1825
500.00	John Meetze & David Hendrix	5th Septr "
2,000.00	James Calk & Amos Banks	7th May " will annexed
5000.00	Judah Barnett & West Coughman	11th Octr "
8000.00	Manuel Corley & West Coughman	26th Augt " this is a second granting the former being revoked
1000.00	John Metz Sr & John Metz Jr.	31st Decr 1825
300.00	Isaac Lybrand & Uriah Pickey	3rd Nov "
		11th Apl "
		9th Septr "
		16th " "
		8th Nov "

Agreeable to an act of the General Assembly of the State hereby Returned the following Memorial of Deeds and other in the office of Register of Mense(sic) for said District to the 1817.

Names of the Parties and their additions	What kind of conveyance	Quantity of land and on what water course
Abner Blocker & others to Nicholas Hane	Bond of indemnity	-- ---
Zilpha Eddins to James & Wm Eddins	Deed	Pine land on waters of Saluda
Evin Howard to Daniel Walker	Deed	waters of Edisto 472 acres
John Shultz to George Caughman	Deed	Saluda waters 110 acres
Jacob Slagle to John Craps	Deed	Congaree River waters 66 acres
James Pou to Henry Ruff	Sheriffs Titles	82 acres waters of of Broad River
Abraham Lansdale to Jesse Fox	Deed	131 acres waters of of Edisto River
David Callaham to Jesse Fox	Deed	150 acres waters of Edisto River
Martin Johnson to Jesse Fox	Deed	300 acres waters of Edisto River
Anthony Adams to Jacob Johnson	Deed	70 acres waters of Edisto River
Joel Hall to Anthony Adams	Deed	4 acres waters of Edisto
John Wing to John Howard	Deed	100 acers waters of Edisto
John Griffin to Anthony Adams	Deed	70 acres waters of Edisto
John Baughman to John Howard	Deed	200 acres waters of Edisto
William Sleigel to George Kaigler	Deed	50 acres waters of the Congaree
John Geiger to George Kaigler	Deed	250 acres on the Congaree River
John Kaigler to George Kaigler	Deed	19½ acres on the Congaree River
Michael Kaigler to George Kaigler	Deed	14½ acres on the Congaree River
Michael Kaigler to George Kaigler	Deed	21 acres on the Congaree River
Michael Kaigler to George Kaigler	Deed	21½ acres on the Congaree River
Henry Shull to Daniel Shull	Deed	3/4th of an acre waters of Saluda

of South Carolina Passed the 17th day of March 1785, I have
Conveyances proved and Recorded in the District of Lexington
office of Secretary of State for the year Ending the first of January

At what time dated	For what consideration	At what time Proved and acknowledged
2d Feby 1816	$1000	17 February 1816
20th Feby 1816	Love	22 Feby 1816
31 octr 1810	$250	24 Feby 1816
29th Augt 1815	$550	26 Feby 1816
21 Feby 1815	$132	27th Feby 1816
8th March 1816	$50	8th March 1816
5th Jany 1815	$50	23 March 1816
3d Feby 1808	$100	23d March 1816
4th Novr 1804	$250	23d March 1816
13th July 1807	$70	26 March 1816
13th July 1807	$30	26 March 1816
12th Jany 1808	$100	27th March 1816
19th Octr 1807	$20	27th March 1816
10th Augt 1815	$150	27th March 1816
day of 1814	$100	28th March 1816
21s May 1811	$200	28th March 1816
6 Septr 1811	$500	29th March 1816
6 Septr 1811	$700	29th March 1816
8th Septr 1802	£ 50	29th March 1816
6 Septr 1811	$800	29th March 1816
13th March 1816	$1	10th April 1816

Names of the Parties and their additions	What kind of conveyance	Quantity of land and on what water course
John Drehr to Henry Wingard	Deed	25 acres on Saluda waters
John Drehr to Henry Wingard	Deed	100 acres on Saluda Waters
West Allen to William Hall	Deed	215 acres waters of Edisto River
Stephen Johnson to Joseph Burgess	Deed	75 acres waters of Edisto
Michael Kaigler to George Kaigler	Deed	18 acres on the Congaree River
John Windle Shealy to Andrew Shealy	Bond for Titles	200 acres of land waters of Saluda
Abner Williams to John W. Lee	a mutual agreemt.	the whole Estate
Frances Saunders to George Creps	Deed	200 acres waters of Saluda River
Adam Amick & others to George Michl Ergle	Deed	50 acres waters of Saluda
Adam Amick & others to Catharine Amick	Deed	50 acres waters of Saluda
Henry Amick & others to Adam Amick	Deed	100 acres waters of Saluda
Adam Amick & others to Henry Amick	Deed	100 acres waters of Saluda
Adam Amick & others to Gasper Amick	Deed	100 acres waters of Saluda
Frances Coon to Adam Amick	Deed	156 acres waters of Saluda
John Gibson to Thomas K. Poindexter	Deed	16½ acres waters of Saluda
Jacob Warne to Henry Summer	Lease & Release	300 Acres Saluda
Henry Summer & wife to Henry Amick	Lease & Release	300 acres on Saluda
John Benedict Mayer to John Adam Epting	Deed	22 3/4 A Broad River
Samul. Ansminger & wife to John Bouknight Junr.	Deed	125 Acres waters of Broad River
Mathias Quattlebom to John Lightner	Deed	450 acres waters of Saluda
John Lightner to William Snelgrove	Deed	250 acres waters of Saluda
William Snelgrove to George Wise	Deed	250 acres Saluda waters
John Shultz to Audeon St. John	Lease & Release	50 acres waters of Saluda

At what time dated	For what consideration	At what time Proved and acknowledged
26st April 1810	$25	11th April 1816
29th Jany 1808	$400	11th Do Do
5th Septr 1812	$600	11th April 1816
30th April 1814	$150	12th April 1816
8th Septr 1802	₤ 90	12th April 1816
4th January 1816	$1000	12th April 1816
10th March 1816	Maintainance	12th April 1816
13th Feby 1815	$200	13th April 1816
day of Jany 1816	$100	15th April 1816
12 January 1816	$100	16th April 1816
12th Jany 1816	$200	16th April 1816
12th Jany 1816	$200	17 April 1816
12th January 1816	$200	17 April 1816
10th October 1799	₤ 25	18th April 1816
19th February 1816	$170	18th April 1816
26 August 1788	₤ 42	18th April 1816
25th January 1798	₤ 72	20th April 1816
1 January 1813	$300	23d April 1816
26 October 1811	$600	24th April 1816
5th September 1806	$500	24th April 1816
29th September 1813	$450	25th April 1816
3d February 1816	550	25th April 1816
27th April 1763	₤ 15	30th April 1816

Names of the Parties and their additions	What kind of conveyance	Quantity of land and on what water course
Christopher Sherb to Audeon St. John	Lease & Release	100 acres waters of Saluda
John Saigoirth to Christopher Sherb	Lease & Release	100 acres Santee River
Simon Taylor to Alexr. B. Stark	Deed	110 acres on Saluda River
Lambert Lance to Alexr. B. Stark	Deed	300 acres on Saluda River
Benjamin Buzbee to Alexr B. Stark	Deed	110 acres on Saluda River
Henry M. Rutledge to James Sanders Guignard	Power of attorney	
Henry M. Rutledge by James S. Guignard to Alexr B. Stark	Deed	250 acres on Saluda & B. River
Danl Mazycke to Alexr B. Stark	Lease & Release	250 acres fork of Broad & Saluda Rivers
J. Christopher Sharp to Saml & John Leaver	Deed	40 acres Saluda
Absalom Hendrix to Saml Wingard	Deed	313 acres waters of Saluda
Asa Delozeair agent for Andrew Dewees to James Boatwright	Deed by order of Court of Equity	150 acres on Saluda
Robert Ballard to John Smith	Deed	100 acres waters of Saluda
James Dellet to James Pou	Commr. Title	1 acre Lot in the Village of Granby
Martha Harris to George & Charles See	Deed	not mentioned
John Craps to Samuel Jumper Senr.	Deed	59 acres on the Congaree River
John Freshley to Christian Freshley	Deed	307 acres waters of Broad River
John Friday to Hargrove Arthur & others	Deed	half acre of land in Granby
Elisha Daniel to William Daniel	Deed Deed	100 acres waters of the Congaree
William Daniel to John McCreless	Deed	100 acres waters of the Congaree
George Wingard to William Wingard	Deed	100 acres waters of Saluda
John Gable to Susana Kennerly	Deed	102½ acres waters of Saluda
Jacob & Michael Rouch to George Derick	Deed	286 acres waters of Saluda

At what time dated	For what consideration	At what time Proved and acknowledged
1st May 1763	₤ 65	7th May 1816
3 September 1755	₤ 100	8th May 1816
13th December 1797	$50	9th May 1816
1 day of Jany 1799	----	9th May 1816
__ day of 1801	$10	9th May 1816
6 September 1805	----	Do Do Do
3d June 1812	$100	Do Do Do
8th Novr 1799	$140	13th May 1816
15th Septr 1812	$49.75	15th Do Do
10th Novr 1815	$100	15th May 1816
3 December 1814	$550	18th May 1816
9th March 1816	$120	20th May 1816
8th April 1816	$395	22 May do
13th Novr 1813	₤ 5	22nd do do
23d Feby 1815	$100	do do do
6 February 1816	$500	23rd May 1815
14th September 1815	Donation	24th May 1816
3d day of April 1813	$300	25th do do
6 Novr 1815	$300	25th do do
28th May 1816	$100	31st May 1816
25th March 1816	$250	Do Do Do
25th Novr 1814	$386	6 June 1816

Names of the Parties and their additions	What kind of conveyance	Quantity of land and on what water course
George Summer to J. Bennedict Mayer	Deed	640 waters of Broad River
Arnold Hutchinson & wife To J. Bennedict Mayer	Deed	Waters of Broad River 27 acres
Samuel Kinard to J. Bennedict Mayer	Deed	27 acres waters of Broad River
Margrate Hallman to J. B. Mayer	Deed	27 acres waters of Broad
Michl. Beadenbaugh to J. B. Mayer	Deed	27 acres waters of Broad River
Nicholas Summer To J. B. Mayer	Deed	241½ acres waters of Broad River
George Summer to J. B. Mayer	Deed	331½ acres waters of Broad River
Wm Sweetonberg To J. Benedict Mayer	Deed	160 acres waters of Broad River
John Hallman To Bennedict Mayer	Deed	100 acres waters of Broad River
George Holddewanger To Thomas S. Herbert	Deed	150 acres waters of Broad River
Henry Seibels (Sheriff) to Bennedict Mayer	Deed	330 acres waters of Broad River
Thomas Herbert To Benedict Mayer	Deed	150 acres waters of Broad River
George Swygert To George Holdewanger	Deed	100 acres waters of Broad River
John Isley To George Swygert	Deed	100 acres Broad River
Nicholas Shular To George Holdewanger	Lease & Release	50 acres waters of Broad River
Frederick Rall To John Snelgrove Junr	Deed	23 acres waters of Saluda
John See to John Snelgrove	Deed	75 acres waters of Saluda
Henry M. Rutledge to John Snelgrove	Deed	100 acres waters of Saluda
George B. Shrum to Lewis Coursey	Lease & Release	100 acres waters of Saluda
Mary Saltzer To Michael Kennemore	Lease & Release	100 acres waters of Saluda
West & George Caughman to Jacob Lites	Deed	100 acres waters of Saluda
Samuel Oswalt To Michael Kennemore	Deed	6 acres waters of Saluda
Lewis Coursey To Adam Saltzer	Lease & Release	100 acres waters of Saluda

At what time dated	For what consideration	At what time Proved and acknowledged
10th Feby 1811	$600	11th June 1816
12th Jany 1816	$250	12 June 1816
14th December 1811	$330	13 Do Do
19th March 1814	$250	Do Do Do
3d June 1811	$210	Do Do Do
13th February 1811	$850	14th Do Do
16th Febry 1811	$800	15th June 1816
16th January 1804	$100	17th Do Do
18th November 1812	$1076	Do Do Do
19th January 1811	$400	Do Do Do
1st March 1816	$1002	18th Do Do
19th January 1811	$500	Do Do Do
18th Jany 1811	$50	19th Do Do
23 February 1787	Five shillings	19th June 1816
27th June 1786	Ten shillings	Do Do Do
7th Feby 1815	$50	20th June 1817
25 June 1805	$100	Do Do Do
7 May 1811	$20	22 Do Do
19th May 1794	℔ 12	26 Do Do
25th June 1814	$110	27th Do Do
17th June 1815	$100	29 Do Do
24th Octr 1808	$50	Do Do Do
22nd Septr 1794	℔ 35	2 July 1816

Names of the Parties and their additions	What kind of conveyance	Quantity of land and on what water course
Lawrence Corley & Wife to Godfrey Harman	Lease & Release	103 acres waters of Saluda
John C. Sharp To David Friday	Deed	272 acres waters of Saluda
Randolph Geiger to Ainsley Hall	Mortgage & Bond	394 acres Congaree River
Needham Davis To Alexr B. Stark	Deed	33 acres on Broad River
Needham Davis to Alexr B. Stark	Right of a road through his land	
Thomas Frick to Caty Frick	Deed	120 acres waters of Saluda
Thomas Frick to Christena Shealy	Deed	78 acres waters of Saluda
Jacob Segrest to David Weaver	Deed	1800 acres waters of Edisto River
Shaderick Beasley to David Weaver	Deed	100 acres waters of Edisto River
Jacob Drafts To Samuel Drafts	Deed	100 acres on Saluda River
John Gable To Mathias Wecker	Deed	167 acres waters of Saluda
George Frey to Philip Martin Frey	Deed	50 acres waters of Saluda
Jacob Jefcoat to Lewis Jones	Deed	118 acres waters of Edisto River
Drewry Boldlin(?) to Mary Leard	Deed	100 acres waters of Edisto River
Michael See to Lewis Carnline	Deed	50 acres waters of Saluda
Lewis Carnline to John Leaphart	Deed	100 acres waters of Saluda
Cristian Caroline to Lewis Carline	Deed	618 acres on Saluda River
Thomas Boyles to John Leaphart	Deed	100 acres Saluda waters
Lewis Carnline to John Leaphart	Deed	50 acres waters of Saluda
Alexander B. Stark to James Kennerly	Deed	260 acres waters of Saluda
David Kennerly & wife to James Kennerly	Deed	133.3½ square chains waters of Saluda
Thomas Rall to James Kennerly	Deed	133 1/3 acres on Saluda
Margaret Slappy to Randolph Geiger	Release of Personal Property	------

27

At what time dated	For what consideration	At what time Proved and acknowledged
17th April 1795	₤ 20	3 July 1816
21 May 1816	$760	5th July 1816
3d December 1814	$8000	11th July 1816
18th July 1816	$330	31st July 1816
18th July 1816	the rights of the Road for the use of the ferry	Do Do Do
3d Septr 1814	Love & good will	15th Augt 1816
3d September 1814	Love & good will	Do Do Do
10th January 1816	$75	16th Augt. 1816
13 April 1816	$100	16th Augt 1816
14 January 1815	$400	Do Do Do
20th May 1816	$450	17th Augt 1816
20th January 1816	$30	Do Do Do
5th July 1815	$55	20th Do Do
16th July 1816	$35	27th Augt 1816
30th September 1808	$150	Do Do Do
19th August 1815	$50	Do Do Do
11th February 1812	blank	28th Do Do
19th Augt 1815	$50	29 Do Do
19th Augt 1815	$50	Do Do Do
29th Decr 1808	$150	Do Do
13th Decr 1808	$933.33	2 September 1816
13th Decr 1811	$533.33	4th September 1816
None		17th Do Do

Names of the Parties and their additions	What kind of conveyance	Quantity of land and on what water course
John McCreless to Jesse W. Rhay	Deed	193 acres waters of Broad River
George Slappy to John Slappy	Bill of Sale	2 Negroes
George Slappy to Jacob C. Slappy	Bill of Sale	one negro lad Joe
James Dellet Commr. in Equity to George Derick	Deed	697 acres waters of Broad River
John Drehr to Ann Shular	Deed of Gift	170 acres Saluda waters 150 Do Do
John Ragnous to John Ferrick	Lease & Release	50 acres waters of Saluda
Jacob Bowers to George Wise	Deed	150 acres waters of Saluda
Henry Seibels (Sheriff) to James S. Guignard	Deed	250 acres waters of Saluda
Henry Seagrest to His Grand Children	2 Deeds of Gift	Cows & Sheep &C &C
Alexr B. Stark to Peter Raimick	Deed	74 acres waters of Broad River
Needham Davis to James S. Guignard	Deed	85 acres Broad River
Peter Redman to Daniel Pound	Deed	196 acres waters of Edisto River
Daniel Jefcoat to Benjamin Jefcoat	Deed	360 acres waters of Edisto River
Jacob Lindler & others to James Dailey	Deed	110 acres waters of Broad River
Rosana Pence & husband to Daniel Drafts	Deed	100 acres Saluda
John Drehr to Daniel Drafts	Do	150 acres Do
William Hall to Arthur Fort	Do	206 acres Edisto waters
John P. Bond to to John Sawyer Senr	Do	605 acres w of Saluda
Ann Lefloor to Martin Free	Do	105 acres waters of Saluda
Joseph Kennerly to Ulrick Coogler	Do	150 acres Sulada (sic)
The Court of Equity to Andrew & Margaret Kaigler	Return in partition	463 acres Congaree River
Christian Rister & wife to Thomas Boyd	Lease & Release	21 acres waters of Broad River
George Stidham to John Haney	Deed	1000 acres Edisto waters

At what time dated	For what consideration	At what time Proved and acknowledged		
23 Augt 1816	$757	12th September 1816		
8th Februry	$428.57	17th	Do	Do
10th January 1811	$428.57	17th	Do	Do
10th August 1816	$242.95	17th	Do	Do
5th January 1813	good will	28th	Do	Do
17th March 1764	₤ 50	2d October		Do
20th April 1816	$150	9th	Do	Do
23d September 1816	$60	Do	Do	Do
18th April 1816	Good will	11th	Do	Do
22d March 1800	₤ 37	24th	Do	Do
	$3140	26	Do	Do
3d Octor 1816	$350	Do	Do	Do
13 May 1816	$80	Do	Do	Do
25th October 1810	$100	29th October 1816		
6 Feby 1810	$200	31 October 1816		
1812	$150	1 Novr		Do
22 December 1808	$200	14th Do		Do
2d October 1816	$500	Do	Do	Do
10th Septr 1816	$120	Do	Do	Do
10th March 1800	₤ 15	18th	Do	Do
	$2062	Do	Do	Do
13th Augt 1794	₤ 21	20th November 1816		
6 January 1815	$80	24th	Do	Do

Names of the Parties and their additions	What kind of conveyance	Quantity of land and on what water course
John Haney to Daniel Jefcoat	Do	Do Do as above
Gasper Amick to Gasper Ellesor	Deed	50 acres Saluda

South Carolina)
Lexington District)

       I John McCreless Register of mesne Conveyance for the District aforesaid, do hereby Ceritfy, that the annexed Sheets contains a Just and true memorial of the Deeds and other Conveyances Recorded in the Registers office for said District for the year Ending the first of January 1817.

                                                      John McCreless   Register

At what time dated	For what consideration	At what time Proved and acknowledged
13 May 1816	$100	24th November 1816
14th Novr 1816	$450	5th January 1817

Agreeable to an act of the General Assembly of the State of South
the following memorial of Deeds and other Conveyances proved and
mense(sic) Conveyance for said District to the office of Secretary

Names of the Parties and their additions	What kind of conveyance	Quantity of land and on what water course
Ainsley Hall to Randolph Geiger	Deed	394 acres Congaree River
John C. Sharp to John David Sharp	Deed	959 acres Broad River
Elizabeth Rish to John A Able	Deed	125 acres Saluda River
Peter Shumperd to Abraham Boland	Deed	150 acres more or less waters of Saluda
John Hall Senr To John Oswalt Junr	Deed	200 acres waters of Lightwood Creek
Peter Miller to M C Taylor	Mortgage	100 acres waters of the Congree
Levi Chaney To John Hufman	Deed	230 acres a branch of Bull Swamp
John David Sharp to Abraham Geiger	Deed	25 acres Broad & & Saluda Rivers
David & Elizh Senn to Josph Airhart	Deed	50 acres Saluda River
Michael Oswalt to Jacob Lites	Deed	100 acres more or less waters of Saluda Ri
George E. Keabler to John Swaigard	Deed	200 acres more or less Saluda River
Joseph Williams to John Sely(?)	Deed	215 acres
Benjmin Hughs to George Long	Deed	128 acres Clouds Creek waters of Saluda
John Levingston to George Long	Deed	250 acres Saluda
Jeremiah Busbee to George Long	Deed	40 acres more or less Saluda
Wm Hughs & Elizh. Rogers to George Long	Deed	137 acres waters of Saluda
Charles Bell to George Long	Deed	204 acres waters of Saluda
George B. Minick to William Minick	Bill of Sale	Cattle & other Personal property
G. B. Minick to William Minick	Deed for life	300 acres Land waters of Broad River
Henry M. Rutledge & James S. Guignard to Lewis Carnline	Deed	703 acres Waters of Saluda
John & Mary Kelly to Anna Richardson	Deed	35½ acres on So side of Saluda

Carolina Passed the 17th day of March 1785. I haveby(sic) Returned Recorded in the District of Lexington in the office of Register of of State for the year Ending the first January 1814.

At what time dated	For what consideration	At what time Proved and acknowledged
2d Decr 1814	$8,000	2d Decr 1814
2 Octr(?) 1813	5 shillings	13th October 1813
21 Septr 1814	$500	24 Septr 1814
5th Augt 1814	$400	1st October 1814
13th Augt 1810	$200	13th Augt 1810
8th Octr 1814	$60	10th October 1814
15th July 1813	$100	21st Augt 1813
28th October 1813	$30	17th May 1814
27th January 1814	$32.50	25 June 1814
22 Novr 1814	$480	26 Novr 1814
9 January 1802	$100	10th February 1802
22 Decr 1813	$600	17 March 1814
25th June 1814	$400	13th August 1814
11th Feby 1794	£ 40	5th July 1794
4th Decr 1810	$85	6th January 1810
5th Jany 1808	$135	5th January 1808
24th Feby 1814	$200	5th March 1814
13th Feby 1814	$100	21st September 1814
13th Feby 1812	Maintainance	21st September 1814
19th Sept 1814	$175.75	28th January 1815
23d Sept 1814	$30	23d Sept 1814

Names of the Parties and their additions	What kind of conveyance	Quantity of land and on what water course
George Slappy to Wm H. Lee	Deed of Gift	2 Negroes
Robert Hails to George Slappy	Bill of Sale	6 negroes
George Slappy to Esaias Saylor & Wife	Deed of Gift	5 Negroes
George Slappy to E. Saylor & Wife & Wm. H. Lee	Bill of Sale	5 Negroes
Thos Boyd to John Jacobs	Deed	4 or 5 acres waters Broad River
Thos Bod(sic) to John McCreless	Deed	192 1/5 acres waters Broad River
Return of the Commissioners appointed to Divide the Estate of Jacob Saylor		249 acres
Elizabeth Hendrix, Henry Hendrix, Saml & David Hendrix & Absolem Hendrix to John Hendrix	Deed	250 acres
Frederick Rister to David Rister, Fredrik Rister & John Jacob Rister	Deed of Gift	Cattle and Horses and other things
Michael Sharp to Abraham Geiger	Deed	242 acres Saluda
Cornelous Clark to George Creps	Deed	300 acres branch Congaree Creek
Jacob Lites to John H. Eifert	Deed	90 acres more or less waters of Horse Creek
Jacob Nees to Danl. & Saml Rambo	Deed	789 acres waters of Edisto River
George B Minick Rosana B. Rish	Deed of Gift	A Negro Girl names Polly
Shearwood Busby to John Bouknight	Lease & Release	111 acres Broad River
Jacob Elesor to John Bouknight	Deed	50 acres more or less Broad River
Jesse Frazer to John Bouknight	Deed	93 acres Broad River
Abner Snelgrove to to John Snelgrove	Deed	93½ acres Campin Creek
William Snelgrove to John Snelgrove	Deed	203½ acres Saluda River
John Snelgrove to Wm Snelgrove	Deed	243 acres Saluda
Abner Snelgrove to Wm Snelgrove	Deed	293½ acres Saluda River
James Patton & Co to Messrs Patton Kelly & Patton	Deed	1/4 of an acre, a Lot in Granby

35

At what time dated	For what consideration	At what time proved and acknowledged
19th Sept 1814	5 shillings	28th Feby 1815
22 Decr 1794	℔ 140	10th Sept 1797
19th Sept 1814	5 shillings	28th Feby 1815
19th Sept 1814	$50	28th Feby 1815
18th July 1805	$16	13th July 1805 (sic)
3d Augt 1813	$400	3d August 1813
------	-----	1808
30th April 1807	$300	30th April 1807
24 Novr 1814	----	26 Novr 1814
29 Sept 1814	$480	27 October 1814
3d June 1814	$235	
22 Novr 1814	$250	15 Decr 1814
1813	$50	25th February 1814
13 Feby 1812	---	20th Sept 1814
2 March 1793	℔ 100	28th Decr 1793
26 March 1803	$100	26 March 1803
17 Decr 1802	$200	26 March 1803
1 July 1814	$10	1 July 1814
1 July 1814	$10	21st July 1814
1st July 1814	$10	21 July 1814
1 July 1814	$10	21st July 1814
7 Decr 1814	$2,000	18th February 1815

Names of the Parties and their additions	What kind of conveyance	Quantity of land and on what water course
Jesse Coryell to Laurence Harman	Deed	200 acres waters of Saluda River
Dennis Gibson to Mary Kennerly	Deed	21 acres waters of Saluda
Samuel Gibson to Mary Kennerly	Deed	62 acres waters of Saluda
Godfrey Harman to Thos K. Poindexter	Deed	125 acres waters of Saluda River
Randolph Geiger to William Geiger	Deed	350 acres on the Congaree River
A. debardelaben to Wm Geiger Senr	ret. for three negros	
Abraham Gieger to Free Heney	Deed	50 acres on Saluda waters
John Freshley to Christian Freshley	Deed	600 acres on Broad River
J. Harman Geiger to Jacob Tyler	Deed	230 acres waters of the Congaree River
Fredrick Wise to George Wise	Deed of Gift	50 acres waters Congaree River
George Bouknight to John Bouknight	Deed	368 acres waters of Broad River
George Bouknight to John Bouknight	Deed	100 acres in Orangeburgh District
Saml Jefcoat to Levy Chany	Deed	240 acres waters of Edisto River
In Equity a bill for Partition Michael Kaiglers Estate		
John Taylor to H. M. Rutledge	Mortgage	18 acres on Saluda River
John Loreman to David Kaigler	Deed	75 acres Congare River
G. B. Minick to Wm Minick	Deed of Gift	Horses and other things
L. W. Threewitts to Joseph W Loyd	Recept	The sum of 4000 for 12 negroes
J. W. Lloyd to L. W. Threewitts	Do	Do
William Boatwright to Lewis Hartley	Deed	63 acres waters of Edisto River
Laurence Crim to John Crim	Deed	one hundred acres Beaver Creek
Michael Deckert to John Fredrick Shaver	Deed	268 acres waters Saluda
Joseph Williams and Richard Williams to John Shely	Bond for Titles to Dower	

At what time dated	For what consideration	At what time proved and acknowledged
3d Feby 1815	$120	17th February 1815
3d March 1809	$105	1st June 1809
3d April 1811	$500	24th October 1813
21 June 1814	$600	22d June 1814
1st Janr 1815	$3,000	22 April 1815
4th Novr 1814	$800	
7th Apl 1814	Love	27th October 1814
5th Octr 1813	$2,000	25th October 1813
14th Jany 1815	$300	13th March 1815
23d Jany 1808	good will	15th January 1815
25 Octr 1811	$736	25th October 1811
2 Augt 1794	₤ 10	31 May 1800
2 Decr 1814	$100	24th April 1815

The Return of the Commissioners

At what time dated	For what consideration	At what time proved and acknowledged
11th Novr 1814	$118	22 February 1815
20 Sept 1814	$350	1st July 1815
13th Feby 1812		15th March 1815
3d March 1813	$4,000	
Do	$4,000	
28th Apl 1814	$60	21 July 1814
14 March 1815	$214.25	14th March 1815
1st Augt 1814	$402	3d Sept 1814
22 Decr 1813	$1,000	

Names of the Parties and their additions	What kind of conveyance	Quantity of land and on what water course
Isaac Lansdale to George Crotwell	Deed	130 acres Hollow Creek
Nicholas Fulmer to George Crotwell	Deed	160 acres Hollow Creek
James Pou Sheriff to Joseph May	Deed	100 acres Broad River
Charles L. Hillman to Jacob Lindler	Deed	160 acres waters of Broad River
Seth & Ester Stone to Thomas & James Turner	Ret.	Legasee(?)
Jacob Tyler to John Geiger Senr	Deed	323 Acres Congaree River
George Stedham & Wife to Jacob Segrest	Deed	1000 acres
John Deckert to Ulrick Wessinger	Deed	100 acres Bear Creek waters of Saluda
John Deckert to Ulrick Wessinger	Deed	109 acres Bear Creek
Mathias Quadlebom to M. & J. DICKERT	Deed	1063 acres Bear Creek
John D. Sharp to Needham Davis	Deed	208 acres between Broad and Saluda Rivers
Michael J. Sharp to Needham Davis	Deed	135 acres in fork of Broad and Saluda Rivers
Jacob Huffman to Needham Davis	Deed	7 acres Broad River
Fredrick Weightenburg to John Black	Deed	130 acres waters of Saluda River
Michael Wise to John Black	Deed	100 acres waters of Saluda River
Ulrick Kyzer to Eberhard Swightenburg	Lease & Release	130 acres waters of Saluda River
Robert Stark to John Taylor	Deed	853 acres on the Congaree River
The Same to the same	Bill of sale	23 negroes & Stock &C &C
James Pou Sheriff to John H. Eiffert	Sheriff Title	657 acres waters of Edisto River
George Hout to Benjn. Cetsinger	Deed	88 acres waters of Broad River
Benjn Geatsinger to James Brooks	Deed	100 acres Broad River
Simeon Elleazer to David Bright	Deed	47 acres more or less Broad River
Elizabeth Broon & others to Jacob Bright	Deed	179 acres Broad River

At what time dated	For what consideration	At what time proved and acknowledged
8th June 1814	$500	25th June 1814
11 July 1814	$300	25th July 1814
15 March 1815	$602	15 March 1815
8th Feby 1815	$25	8th Feby 1815
15 July 1814	1 negro & $210	11th August 1814
14th Janay 1815	$5,000	13th March 1815
26 July 1814	$150	13 March 1815
4th Feby 1815	$200	10th Feby 1815
23 October 1813		23d Octr 1813
22 Sept 1810	$2,000	22 Sept 1810
16th Feby 1815	$2,100	13th May 1815
1st Augt 1813	$400	2 Septr 1815
13th Augt 1814	$78	7th November 1815
15th May 1815	$150	15th May 1815
13th Sept 1815	$50	9th October 1815
6 Decr 1792	₤ 50	29th Decr 1792
13th Octr 1815	$15,000	16th October 1815
13th Octr 1815	$15,000	16th October 1815
7th Augt 1815	$21.12	20th October 1815
20th Feby 1808	$350	20th Febry 1808
14th Feby 1802	$100	16th January 1802
7th Novr 1814	$40	7th Novr 1814
25th Septr 1813	$550	7th October 1813

Names of the Parties and their additions	What kind of conveyance	Quantity of land and on what water course
Wm. H. Geiger to George Kaigler	Deed	350 acres Congaree River
Thos Herbert & Wife to Geo. Stoudemeyer	Deed	431 acres Broad River
Esaias Say & Wife & Wm. H. Lee to Uriah & Reuben Hayly Slappy	Deed of Gift	of five negroes
G. B. Minick to John Minick	Deed of Gift	one negroe
James Boyd to Davis Austin	Deed	753 acres waters of Saluda
Joseph Hallman to Davis Austin	Deed	330 acres more or less waters of Saluda
Nicholas Vanzant to Mathias Oswalt	Lease for a term of 7 years	40 acres waters of Saluda River
Wm Snelgrove Sheriff to John P. Bond	Sheriffs Title	75 acres waters of Saluda River
Wm. Jones to Susannah and Ellener King	Deed	300 acres more or less Black Creek
George J. Strother to Christian Harman	Deed	105 acres Saluda River
George Setzler to Henry Ruff	Deed	12½ acres waters Broad River
Abram Stack Lewis & Jacob Stack	Deed of Gift	125 acres with some stock
Mary Strother to George Aull	Deed	42 acres waters of Saluda
Wm Jones to Shaderick Beesley	Deed	100 acres waters of Edisto River
John Drehr to Valentine Gable	Deed	314 acres on Saluda River
John Carnline to John Shultz and Absalom Hendrix	Deed	100 acres Big Hollow Creek
Eliza, Ann, & Rebeckah Simons to Wm. M. Simons	Power of attorney	
Jacob Epting Senr. to George Stoudemeyer	Deed	100 acres on Broad River
Jesse Fox to Charles Bell	Deed	100 acres on the waters of Edisto
David Williams to David Risinger	Deed	50 acres waters of Saluda
Henry Oswalt & wife to John Wilson	Deed	50 acres waters of Saluda
Lewis Carnline to Martin Free	Deed	60 acres waters of Saluda

At what time dated	For what consideration	At what time proved and acknowledged
1 Septr 1815	$3,000	24th October 1815
8th March 1796	₤ 150	8th March 1796
20th Sept 1814	$5	1st July 1815
13th Febry 1815	good will	30th May 1815
8th Feby 1815	$350	30th May 1815
20th June 1814	$775	20th June 1814
22d Decr 1810		2d February 1816
22d Decr 1814	$100	22d July 1815
5th May 1815	$200	28th July 1815
2d July 1814	$2,000	16th March 1815
5th July 1815	$98	4 July 1815
14th Augt 1815	Good will	
30th Decr 1813	$100	24th Sept 1814
27th Octr 1814	$20	16th November 1814
1st Feby 1806	$60	22 March 1806
28th Augt 1815	$60	6 September 1815
2 Apl 1813	confidence	March 10th 1815
7th Decr 1798	₤ 10	4 July 1801
2 March 1814	$300	21st May 1814
2d Augt 1810	$100	2d Augt 1810
19th Novr 1812	$90	25 Decr 1812
26 Augt 1815	$50	1 Septr 1815

Names of the Parties and their additions	What kind of conveyance	Quantity of land and on what water course
Mathias Folmer & others Nicholas Herring	Deed	66½ acres on Broad River
Richard Tutt to Gabriel H. Tutt	Power of attorney	
Gabriel H. Tutt to Micajah Martin	Recept	for the third part of Land belonging to J. Williams, Decd.
Samuel Jefcoat to John Hooker	Deed	100 acres waters of Edisto River
John Hooker to John Redmond	Deed	100 acres waters Edisto River
David Hendrix to Wm See	Deed	10 acres waters of Saluda
Ulrick Baughman to Jacob Drafts	Deed	150 acres waters Saluda River
Levi Williams to Daniel Wingard	Deed	100 acres on Saluda River
Christopher Sharp to Samuel Huffman	Deed	40 acres Broad River
Wm Arthur & Wife to Joseph Kershaw	Release	175 acres Congaree

At what time dated	For what consideration	At what time proved and acknowledged
29 Decr 1812	$210	4 Decr 1815
17 Augt 1813		17th Augt 1813
26 Octr 1814(1812?)	$417	24th Novr 1815
22d Decr 1801	£ 10	7 Apr 1812
13 Feby 1802	£ 10	7 Apr 1812
26 Decr 1815	$20	26 Decr 1815
25 Decr 1815	$112.50	25th Decr 1815
4th May 1813	$400	28th October 1813
17th Decr 1808	$260	23d Decr 1808
1st May 1777	10 shillings	3d Decr 1801

Agreeable to an act of the General Assembley of the State
I have hereby Returned the following Memorial of
in the District of Lexington in the office of Register
of Secretary of State for the year Ending the first of

Names of the parties and their additions	What kind of conveyance	Quantity of the land and on what water course
Michael Wise Junr to John Huffman	deed	685 acres
Stephen Williams to John Black	Conveyed by Indenture	69 acres on Hollow creek Saluda
Mary Hill to John Black	Deed	54 acres on Hollow creek Saluda
Baroned Lybrand to Jacob Taylor	Deed	170 acres on Horse creek waters of Saluda
Regina Schlis to John Lowerman	deed	100 acres Big John Creek waters of Saluda
John See to Abraham Harris	deed	155 on little creek Congaree River
John W Vanzant to Mathias Oswalt	deed	95 acres Hollow creek waters of Saluda

[columns change here]

Names of the parties	Kind of conv.	Consideration
Susanah See to Henry See	deed	$50
John Kedle(?) and Polly his wife, James Eitson and Elizabeth his wife William Perey and Nancy his wife Sally Blakely to George Moutz	deed	37
William Lybrand to John Snelgrove	deed	188
David Hoke to John Bauknight	deed	50
Zachariah Norts(?) to Jno Bauknight	----	1000
Jno Bauknight to Wm Geiger	deed	100
John Baughman to William Geiger	deed	$40
John Geiger to James Rogers	receipt	$75
H. J. Boughman to Wm Boughman	deed	120
Ezekeal Allman to John Geiger	deed	10 £
Gabl Clements to John Geiger	deed	10 £

of South Carolina passed the 17th day of March 1785
Deeds and other conveyances proved and Recorded
or Mesne conveyance for the Said District to the office
January 1819

At what time dated	For what consideration	At what time proved and acknowledged
22d Novr 1817	$85	16 January 1818
24 Decr 1816	$170	30th April 1817
20 Decr 1816	150	30th April 1817
18 Decr 1815	250	18th May 1816
22nd July 1814	150	26th August 1814
14 Octr 1813	25	17th January 1818
11th Decr 1815	100	15th May 1816

[columns change here]

Quantity of land	What time dated	What time proved & ack.
72 acres on Saluda River	25th Octr 1808	25th Octr 1818
100 acres on Six Mile Creek	-----	---------
12 Island of Saluda River	18th August 1817	14 Septr 1817
78 acres fork Broad & Saluda Rivers	11th Feby 1813	17th Decr 1817
100 Broad River	? Decr 1815	11th December 1817
632 South side of the Congaree Creek	3rd Jany 1818	17th Jany 1818
632 So S of Congaree River	11th Feby 1813	10th Feby 1813
3 acres	17th Jany 1817	25th Octr 1817
150	29 March 1817	29th March 1817
100	29 Nov 1798	2nd May 1815
100 Congaree Creek hollow pond	11 June 1737	21st June 1797

Names of the Parties	Kind of Conveyance	Consideration
Abraham Gieger to John Geiger	Lease & Release	₺ 300
Abram Harris Dorethy Harris Martha Harris George Harris George See Elizabeth Crout John See John Harris & wife Sally See & David Stotes(?) to Harmon & Wm Geiger	deed	$350 each
Jacob Snider to Jacob Rall	deed	150
James Pou to Lewis Pou & Henry Seibels	deed	1450
John Duke to Abm Geiger	deed	150
John Souter to Michael Lorick	deed	350
The same to the same	do	450
Gasper Souter to John Souter	do	100
The same to Michl Lourick	do	300
John Swicard to The Same	do	330
George Lorick to Michael Lorick	Deed	$2000
Joseph Souter to John Souter	deed	100
Christian Sharp to Gasper Souter	do	246
Henry M. Rutledge by his attorney J. S. Guignard to Andrew Tarrar	do	35
Margaret Hampton to George Eigleberger	do	1460
John Drehr, Hannah Hendix Henry Hendrix to Christian Kyzer	do	245
Henry See to the same	do	224
John Hallman, Michael Peterbough to Margaret Hollman	do	70

47

Quantity of land and on what water course	What time dated	What time proved and acknowledged
2560 Congaree Creek	1790 January 9	do do
256 Toms Creek	12 Jany 1818	12th Jany 1818
116 acres Beaver dam creek	March 20th 1809	20th March 1809
lot in the village Granby	18th Decr 1817	26th January 1817(sic)
500 North Edisto	3r day Decr 1810	7th Decr 1817
fork B & S River 49	11th Feby 1817	26 April 1817
do 34	do 1817	26th April do
f B & S River 49½ do	14 Augt 1816	22nd January 1818
N Side Saluda 2 acres	9th March 1811	4th do 1817
100 low down in the fork of B & S	9th Septr 1816	26th April 1817
250 acres S side Saluda	8th March 1811	4th January 1817
34 acres N Side do	14th Augt 1816	22nd Jany 1818
59¾ acres do f B & S Rivers	30th Decr 1811	26 April 1817
136 do	4th feby 1808	11 feby 1819
246 do B River	26th Novr 1816	28th feby 1818
100 do S side Saluda	----	----
208 do Beachcreek Sal.	12th day Decr 1815	12th Decr 1815
two 6th parts of one hundred acres waters of B. River	7th Nov 1813	30 Nov 1815

Names of the Parties	Kind of Conveyance	Consideration
Ainey Hutchison to John Enlow	Deed	35
Charles Bundrick to Spence Morgan	Lease & release	Ł 5
James Beard & wife to the same	do	70 Ł
Simon Eleazer to the Same	Released	15 Ł
The same to the same	do	3 Ł
Christian Long & wife to Andrew Holman	do	10 S
Charles Williamson to Peter Redman	Deed	130
Benjamin Busby to Henry Kunkle	do	200
Henry Weaver to John Lee	do	100
John Oswalt to Michael Wingard	do	250
John Lee to Michael Wingard	do	150
John Rouf to Godfrey Roof	do	---
Benjamin Roof to Godfrey Roof	do	----
Michael Erigle to Joseph Lites	do	80
Frederick Kelly to Joseph Lites	do	180
Susanna Snider to William Dent	do	500
John Hendrix to Thos K. Poindexter	do	650
James Dellet Esqr. Comr in Equity to The Same	Release	175
John Benton to Amos Banks	deed	312
Jacob Fullmer to John Benton	do	160
Drusiller Brasilman Exr. to Henry Muller	deed	$600
Mathias Wicker to Susanah Lyles	do	820
Amos Banks Shff (James Erwin) to Nicholas Hane	Sheriff Title	55

Quantity of land and on what water course	What time dated	What time proved and acknowledged
one sixth part 100 acres do	13th Novr 1813	do
100 do fork B & S	6th Jany 1801	15th Septr 1802
100 do waters of River (Broad?)	13 May 1794	------
30 do S side of Broad River	6th April 1798(?)	13th June 1799
do	19th Nov 1792	29 Octr 1816
waters of B River 100 acres	26th day Decr 1794	18th December 1817
300 acres on Big pond N Edisto	3rd October 1816	3rd Octr 1816
50 acres wateree creek	4th April 1806	18th October 1806
420 acres	16th October 1817	20 Octr 1817
612 acres Twelve Mile Creek	29th October 1817	3rd Nov 1817
420 acres Twleve mile Creek	18th Octr 1817	20th Octr 1817
165 acres S side Saluda	20th April 1811	14th June 1811
50 acres waters of Twelve Mile Creek	7th day of Feby 1816	7th feby 1816
521 acres Bear Creek	14th August 1817	14th August 1817
34 acres	1st August 1816	28th Octr 1816
700 acres on Branches of Rocky Creek	25 Feby 1817	24th Decr 1817
120 acres on Twenty mile and 12 mile Creek Branches	17th Nov 1816	15th March 1817
200 acres on fourteen mile branch	1816	3rd day of January 1817
50 acres Cutlog Creek	29th Novr 1817	4th Decr 1817
50 acres Saluda waters	28th Decr 1811	23rd Decr 1811
704 acres on Congaree Creek	9th day of feby 1818	23rd march 1818
167 acres on Kenerlys Creek	20 October 1817	26th feby 1817
480 Laying on Bull Swamp Creek	11th April 1818	23rd April 1818

Names of the Parties	Kind of Conveyance	Consideration
The Same to The Same	do	100
Samuel Oswalt to Christian Lightner	deed	500
Thomas Fox Junr to Jesse Fox	do	125
James Boatright to Jacob Nonemaker	do	120
Jacob Jefcoat & John Hooker to Simon Redman	do	85
Henry Lewy to Frederick Ellesor	do	300
John Friday to Nicholas Hane	do	700
John Hogg to Jacob Turnipseed Junr	do	1200
The Same to Jacob Turnipseed of Fairfield	do	1250
Amos Banks Esq to Jacob Kinard	Sheff Title	90
Abraham Fulmer to James Dayly	deed	----
Christian Swigart to Jacob Rice	do	100
George Golden Jacob Rice	do	250
Simpson Sawyer to Capt. A. H. Fort & Ansel Sawyer	Deed	$300
John Matheson to John W. Lee	do	45
Mathias Snider to John Snider	do	200
John Snider & Abraham Sandford & Nicholas See, George Snider, William Sanford, Susanah & Sophia Snider to Mathias Snider	do	2000
Jacob Snider to John Snider	do	50
Margaret Younginer, George Younginer, Catherine Gross and George Gross to Sebastian Younginer	do	525
Margaret Timmerly, Eve Margaret Timmerly, John Nicholas to Sebastian Younginer	do	466

Quantity of land and on what water course	What time dated	What time proved and acknowledged
150 on Congaree Creek	14th April 1818	23rd April 1818
100 on Horse Creek	27th January 1817	29 October 1817
100 acres between the 2 Shurlys branches	19th March 1818	26 March 1818
274 waters of Broad River	5th September 1817	5th September 1817
250	1812	8th day June 1812
100 Hollingshead Creek	2nd February 1805	10th May 1805
12 on Mile Creek	23rd April 1818	23rd April 1818
126 on waters of Broad River	27th Septr 1816	6th Decr 1817
40 acres fork of Broad & Saluda Rivers	27th Septr 1816	6th Decr 1817
441 Holly Creek waters of Saluda	4th May 1818	5th May 1818
11 3/4 waters of the Wateree Creek	21st Feby 1818	21 Feby 1818
25 Holly Creek	13th feby 1818	11 April 1818
50 acres do	1st January 1818	22nd Jany 1818
713 acres on the District Line of Lexg. & Edged.	14 Feby 1817	25th Septr 1817
200 do Lightwood Creek waters	8th August 1817	4th Septr 1817
140 acres on waters B Saluda	12th Novr 1817	21st Nov 1817
140 Rockey creek waters of Saluda River	27th June 1814	16th Augt 1814
125 acres on waters of Saluda	10th Septr 1810	10 September 1810
75 Saluda waters	3 Septr 1811	27 April 1812
33 1/3 acres on waters of Saluda	14 January 1815	8th June 1816

Names of the Parties	Kind of Conveyance	Consideration
Jacob Geiger to Sebastian Younginer	do	80
William Harmon to Henry Dominick	do	800
Amos Banks to William Snelgrove	Sheriff Titles	2
Elizabeth Kaigler to David Kaigler	deed	20
the same to the same	do	1500
do do to do do	do	do
Elizabeth Kaigler to David Kaigler	deed	400
Elizabeth Kaigler to David Kaigler	do	2500
the Same to the Same	do	1000
David Kaigler to Elizabeth Kaigler	do	1125
The Same to the Same	do	2125
do do to do do	do	400
do do to do do	do	370
Henry Oswalt & wife to George Oswalt	do	20
the Same to the Same	do	200
Christian Lightner to Drury Sawyer	do	500
Amos Banks Esqr to James Pou	Sheriff Titles	191 cents
Micajah Martin, Joel & Agner Williams to George D. Lesler	accomplisure of partition	$1
the same to John W. Lee	deed of Gift	00
John W. Lee to the Heirs of Jos Williams	do	oo
John Hall Senr to John Mathison	deed	100
Amos Banks Esqr to William Snelgrove	Sheriff Titles	--

53

Quantity of land and on what water course	What time dated	What time proved and acknowledged
13 fork of B & S Rivers	30th Decr 1816	25 Octr 1817
300 waters of Saluda	22nd Feby 1817	22nd Feb 1817
172 unknown where	12 December 1817	2 June 1818
10 acres on the Branches of Sandy Run Creek	25 October 1817	30th May 1818
quantity unknown on the Congaree River	do	do
288 on Sandy Run Creek	do	do
200 acres little Sandy Run	25 October 1817	30 May 1818
30 acres west side Congaree River	do	do
100 do do	do	do
47 acres in Saxegotha now Lexington	do	do
87 acres Congaree River	do	do
100 acres waters of Sandy Run Creek	do	do
185 acres Sandy Run Creek	do	do
136 acres on Beaver Creek Saluda	19 Nov 1812	25th December 1812
200 do Howllow Creek	24 March 1818	2nd April 1818
100 do do	27th January 1817	29th September 1817
237 do on the Columbia Road	15th April 1817	1st July 1818
2535 acres waters of hollow Creek	23rd May 1818	do
567 acres do	do	do
2534 do do	do	do
200 in Lexing. District	25 January 1817	24th April 1817
700 do do	6th July 1818	6th July 1818

Names of the Parties	Kind of Conveyance	Consideration
Gasper Souter to Jacob Souter	deed	74
James Kennerly to Gasper Souter	deed	$26
Gasper Souter to Jacob Strupe for John Mathias Saveur(?)	deed	Ł 20
Gabriel Friday to William Kinsler	do	250
James Dellet Esqr Comr Equity to Jesse M. Howell	Title by the court	----
Theophilus Wilson & wife to John Snelgrove Senr	Deed	100
Abraham Geiger Senr to Gasper Souter	?? of a bargain	150
John Souter to Martin Hook	Deed	750
Samuel Lever to John Souter	do	600
Robert Duke to Henry Muller	do	50
James Dellet Esqr. Comr in Equity to Randolph Geiger	Title in partition ?? of a Bill	3270
John & Ann Harris to Abraham Geiger	deed	75
John Smith to William Daniel	do	350
James Watt to John Watt	do	1600
John Watt to Jacob Rall	do	4000
William Seibels to John Bauknight	do	272.50cts.
Michael Hentz to Sarah Bates	deed	700
Richard Ratcliff to Harmon Geiger & William Geiger	do	200
John T. Seibels to John Uriah Coogler	do	64
Peter Hendrix to Jacob Lites	do	556
Michael Kinamon to John S. Addy	do	362½
John Black to George Croutwell	do	610

Quantity of land and on what water course	What time dated	What time proved and acknowledged
175 acres waters of Saluda River	9th April 1816	27th July 1816
260 acres on waters of Saluda	10 day of April 1813	4 day of January 1817
8 acres on the North side Saluda	25th October 1817	22nd January 1818
320 acres on waters of Six Mile Creek	15th July 1818	15th July 1818
4770½ acres Congaree River &C	24th March 1818	21st April 1818
150 acres on Hollow Creek	23rd day of March 1818	23d March 1818
152 acres on lick Branch waters of Congaree Creek	7 March 1813	3rd August 1818
60 acres more or less on Saluda River	29th January 1817	26th May 1817
60 acres do do	10th October 1815	4th January 1817
837 acres on Congaree River	17th June 1817	17th June 1817
30 Acres Lexington District	3rd August 1818	18th Augt 1818
55 acres more or less	11 february 1813	18th August 1818
100 acres South side	6th April 1818	6th April 1816(sic)
287 acres on Rockey Creek wts. of Saluda	28th December 1818	21 July 1818(sic)
575 do	1st July 1818	23 July 1818
555 acres in the fork of Saluda and Broad Rivers	10th July 1818	22nd July 1818
159 acres waters of N Edisto	5th August 1818	22nd August 1818
925 acres in Orangeburgh District on a Creek called South Edisto River	21st Septr 1818	21st Septr 1818
119 do fork of Saluda & Broad Rivers	25th day Augt 1818	25th Augt 1818
85 acres Lexington	14th August 1818	21st Septr 1818
100 acres Hollow Creek	17th January 1818	14 february 1818
123 acres Hollow Creek	12th February 1818	12th feburary 1818

Names of the Parties	Kind of Conveyance	Consideration
William Hendrix to David Hendrix	do	300
Henry Weaver to David Hendrix	do	410
Henry Seibels to John Metz	do	450
Jacob Drafts to Daniel Drafts	do	700
Adam Emick & Christian Emick to John Summer	do of Gift	---
John Nicholas Senr to Jacob Souter	deed	560
The same to the Same	do	400
Jesse W Rhay to John Rooks	do	20
G D Lester & Abner & Joel Williams to Micajah Martin	do for Division	1
Peter Redman to John Levingston	Deed	$200
John Hoover to John Levingston Senr	do	200
John Summer to Henry T. Crumpton	do	200
Frederick Class to John Wolf	do	850
John Tyler to Frederick Class	lease and release	$10
Mary Gartman to Dennis Hays	do her share	$2.6.66cts
The same to David Gartman	do	100
Phillip Hook & wife to John C. Sharp	deed	$5
Henry Seibels Esqr to Jeremiah Walker	Sheriff Titles	$7
John Miller to Jacob Huffman	Deed	120
Mathias Wessinger to the Same	do	34
Susanah Wessinger, Eve Gough, Fred Bough to the Same	do	110
John Wessinger & wife the Same	do	70

57

Quantity of land and on what water course	What time dated	What time proved and acknowledged
77 acres Beach creek	3rd January 1817	4th February 1916
100 acres Rocky Creek Saluda	11th day July 1815	22rd July 1818
600 acres fork of B & S	26th Septr 1818	3rd October 1818
37 acres Saluda	28th February 1818	4 Octr 1818
100 acres Broad River	27th December 1818	3rd January 1818
50 acres waters of Saluda	-- October 1818	12th October 1818
94 acres waters do	3rd October	12th Octr
2 acres fork Charleston Road	4th October 1817	6th December 1817
1400 acres Hollow Creek	25th day May 1818	12th Octr 1818
200 acres Big pond branch	5th feb 1818	14 March 1818
207 acres do	14 Feb 1818	do
124 acres Orangeburgh	9 April 1817	1st Septr 1818
100 acres Savana ?	4th Novr 1818	7th November 1818
100 do do	8th August 1794	--------
her share of 200 acres	18th April 1817	--------
do of Two hundred acres	17th May 1810	--------
135½ acres	24th April 1816	24th April 1817
400 acres Cedar Creek	2nd Novr 1816	5th Nov 1818
forty acres fork of B & S	3rd Decr 1815	17 April 1817
11 acres do	20 April 1818	1st Septr 1818
100 acres waters of S River	6th June 1814	6 July 1814
their share of 50 acres	28th June 1814	5th do do

Names of the Parties	Kind of Conveyance	Consideration
Needham Davis to the Same	do	28
Saml Fleming, B Smith to John Drehr	do	850
John Drehr to Andrew Kaigler	deed	850

Quantity of land and on what water course	What time dated	What time proved and acknowledged
7 acres	13th Augt 1814	17 April 1817
198 acres Stoney branch waters of S River	6th July 1816	6th July 1816
198 acres Stoney branch waters of Saluda	1st Nov 1816	12 February 1818

Agreeable to an Act of the General Assembley of the State
I have hereby Returned the following Memorial of Deeds
of Lexington in the office of Register of Mesne Conveyance
January 1818

Names of the parties and their additions	What kind of conveyance	Quantity of land and on what water course
William Hendrix to Yost Metz	Deed	127 acres waters of Saluda
Jacob & Michael Smoke to Daniel Kreps	deed	115 acres Johns Creek waters of Saluday
Sarah Seibels to Ryner a free negro	Bill of sale	---------
Christian Rister to John Adam Rister	deed	100 acres on the wateree Creek Saluda waters
Michael Rouch to Samuel Wingard	deed	180 acres branch of high hill Creek Saluda waters
George Wingart to Samuel Wingart Jur.	deed	152 acres on 12 mile creek waters of Saluda
Jacob Bickley to Samuel Wingart	Deed	220 acres Beards Creek Saluda Waters
Christine Hoke to William Hoke	Deed of Gift	land & other property
James Dellet to John Stack	Commissioners Deed	144 acres waters of Saluda
Charles Harrison to Michael Plimail	agreement to make a deed	100 acres
John H. Boughman to John Geiger	deed	50 acres Congaree River
John Wolfe to John Geiger	deed	250 acres Congaree River
John Baughman to John Geiger	deed	3 acres on Congaree River
Lueisa Pinckney & Elizabeth Bellinger to Michael Eragle	deed	500 acres on Bear Creek Saluda
Richard Bartin to William Scofield	deed	40 acres lightwood Creek Edisto River
Daniel Shotts & David Shotts to Andrew Tarror	Deed	132 acres 12 mile Creek
George Metz to Church Wardens	Deed	17 acres between Broad & Saluda Rivers
Yost Metz to Emanuel Corley	Deed	182 acres on S side Saluda River
John D. Sharp to John C. Sharp	Deed	593 acres in the fork of Broad & Saluda Rivers
Hanah Rives to Simon Rives & others	Deed of Gift	Number of negroes
Richard Hampton to Thomas Bartlet	Lease & Release	100 acres on Six mile Creek Congaree waters

of South Carolina Passed the 17th day of March 1785
and other conveyances prooved and Recorded in the District
for said District for the year Ending the first of

At what time dated	for what consideration	At what time proved and Recorded
2nd Octr 1816	$400	5 Jany 1817
12th Novr 1814	$100	8th Jany 1817
14th Jany 1817	$100	14th Jany 1817
7th Decr 1816	$300	28th Jany 1817
16th Jany 1815	$400	30th Jany 1817
18th Feby 1804	$20	Jany 30th 1817
15 day of 37th year of Independence	$800	31st January 1817
25th June 1816	Love & Affection	2d February 1817
10th Augt 1816	$60	15th February 1817
without date	---	proved 1 Day April 1813 Recorded 15th July 1817
st Decr 1803	$200	27th Feby 1817
)th Augt 1811	$700	27th Feby 1817
-- July 1813	$50	27th February 1817
7th Decr 1816	$700	28th Feby 1817
st Novr 1802	$20	28th Feby 1817
st Feby 1812	---	10th March 1817
th Feby 1817	$42(?)	18th March 1817
1st Octr 1816	$400	18th March 1817
8th May 1816	$593	21 March 1817
12th Octr 1816	love & affection	22d March 1817
10th March 1791	10 shillings	26th March 1817

Names of the parties and their additions	What kind of conveyance	Quantity of land and on what water course
John C. Sharp to James S. Guignard	deed	47½ acres on Broad River waters
Friday Arthur as Sheriff to Jacob Baughman	deed	75 acres on the Congaree River
William Kinsler to Emanuel Friday	Deed of Gift	640 acres on Congaree waters
James Boatwright to Jacob Nounamaker	Deed	91 acres on Broad River
John D. Sharp to Jacob Nounemaker	Deed	30 acres on Broad River
James Boatwright to Jacob Huffman	Deed	36 acres on Broad River
Elizabeth Symons, Ann Havis, Rebecca Jackson & William M. Symonds to Needham Davis	deed by power of attorney	250 acres on Broad River
Rebecca Haring to Uriah Mayer	Deed	21 acres on the waters of Broad River
Drucilla Braselman to Michael Bouknight	Deed	423 acres on waters of Saluda
Charles Pellam to James H. Millard	Deed	350 acres on Edisto waters Gleasens(?) branch
James H. Millard to David Gissendanner	Deed	467 acres on Edisto waters
Michael Sharp to John C. Sharp	Deed	240 acres in the fork of Broad and Saluda Rivers
Henry Boozer & others to David Boozer	Deed	196 acres on little Rocky Creek
Nicholas & Nancy House to Solomon Martin	Deed	336 acres on a branch of N Edisto River
Susanah Kenerly to Rachel C. Kennerly	Deed	102½ acres on waters of Kennerly's Creek Saluda waters
Cornelius Clark to Gabriel Friday	deed	444 acres waters of Congaree River
John Hall to Jacob Hall	Deed	200 acres on Marlers branch Edisto waters
John Williams to William Hendrix	deed	100 acres on Rocky Creek Saluda waters
Henry Hendrix to William Hendrix	deed	77 acres on beach Creek Saluda waters
Henry Hendrix to William Hendrix	deed	3 acres twenty mile Creek Saluda R
Jacob Corley & John Shultz William Hendrix	deed	6 acres 20 mile Creek Saluda Waters
Godfrey Roof to Benjamin Roof	Deed	52 acres on waters of Saluda River

At what time dated	for what consideration	At what time proved and Recorded
2d March 1817	---	28th March 1817
8th July 1809	$200	31st March 1817
15th June 1814	love & affection	15th April 1817
9th Apl 1817	$910	16th April 1817
7th Apl 1817	$215	16th Apl 1817
9th Apl 1817	$460	16 Apl 1817
4th March 1817	$one Dollar	17th April 1817
9th March 1817	$200	17th April 1817
20th Jany 1817	$400	18th April 1817
26 Novr 1814	$200	21 April 1817
12th June 1816	$200	21 April 1817
4th June 1816	$1	22d April 1817
1st Octr 1816	$550	22d April 1817
25 Jany 1817	$100	28th April 1817
13th Feby 1817	$250	30th April 1817
4th Feby 1816	$100	Recorded 30th April 1817
2d March 1812	$200	1st May 1817
7 Septr 1816	$550	6 May 1817
23 Sept 1815	$300	6 May 1817
5 Feby 1814	$9	6 May 1817
18th Septr 1811	$18	6 May 1817
15th Jany 1816	---	6 May 1817

Names of the parties and their additions	What kind of conveyance	Quantity of land and on what water course
Thomas Burket to to Jacob Busby	deed	66½ acres on Broad River in the fork
Thomas Burket to Jacob Busby	Deed	82 acres on busby branch Broad River
Philip Touber & wife to Magdalena George	Release	100 acres on Saluda river or near
Michael Stock & Christena Stock to Lutherick George	deed	40 acres on Saluda River or near it
Lewis George to John J. Swicard	Deed	100 acres on Saluda River
Michael Dickert & John Dickert to Henry Ruff	Deed	340 acres on bear Creek Saluda waters
Michael Stock to Henry Ruff	Deed	100 acres on bushes branch
James Hall to John Hall	Deed	273 acres on marlers branch, Edisto waters
Jacob Hall to John Sawyer	Deed	273 acres on Edisto waters
William(?) Hendrix(?) to John Hendrix	Deed	27 acres on 20 mile Creek waters of Saluda River
Jacob Boozer to John Hendrix	deed	193 acres on beaver cam Creek Saluda
John Quattlebom to Michael Barr	Deed	334 acres on lick Creek waters of Saluda
Jeremiah Edwards to Dunsey Coward	Deed	150 acres on Pedbank Creek Congaree Waters
Mary Wing to Daniel Boatwright	Deed	100 acres on Lightwood Creek waters of N Edisto
Daniel Boatwright to William Scofield	Deed	100 acres on lightwood Creek waters of N Edisto River
James Dougharty to George Lindler	Deed	150 acres on the waters of bear Creek Saluda waters
James Dailey & others to George Lindler	Deed	100 acres on Wateree Creek waters of Broad River
Nicholas Hane to Abraham Geiger	Deed	50 acres on Pools Creek
William Snelgrove to Nicholas Hane	Sheriffs Titles	50 acres on Pools Creek waters of Congaree River
Daniel Ravenell to Paul Mazyck	Lease & Release	250 acres in the fork of Broad & Saluda Rivers
Gabriel Fridig to William Kinsler	Deed	444 acres on Redbank waters of the Congaree
Christian Lightner to William Brasill	Deed	100 acres on Six mile Creek
William Brasill to John Harman	Deed	100 acres on 6 mile mile Creek

At what time dated	For what consideration	At what time proved and Recorded
4th Decr 1816	$400	7 May 1817
4th Decr 1816	$217½	7th May 1817
2d Feby 1797	₤ 20 sterling	8th May 1817
16th Augt 1806	$100	8 May 1817
24th Novr 1806	$400	Recorded 8 May 1817
15th Novr 1811	$340	9 May 1817
11th Augt 1810	$350	9 May 1817
26 Sept 1809	$100	9 May 1817
6 Decr 1816	$200	10th May 1817
3d Jany 1816	$80	12th May 1817
2d Novr 1806	$100	12th May 1817
9th July 1816	$1200	12th May 1817
20th June 1816	$150	12th May 1817
2 Feby 1813	$80	13 May 1817
5th March 1813	$80	13 May 1817
18 Decr 1809	$150	13th May 1817
7th Decr 1816	$200	13th May 1817
5th April 1816	$100	14th May 1817
11th June 1814	$100	14 May 1817
15 May 1775	----	28th May 1817
16 May 1817	$600	4 June 1817
9th Novr 1802	$1	5 June 1817
10th March 1804	$200	5th June 1817

Names of the parties and their additions	What kind of conveyance	Quantity of land and on what water course
James Pou to Thomas Rall	Sheriffs Titles	100 acres on 6 mile Creek
John Hall Junr & John Hall Senr to Levy Oswalt	Deed	600 acres on hellhole Creek Edisto waters
Martin Free to Honorious Riddle	Deed	60 acres on Holler Creek waters
Henry Dozer & wife to the Congregation of St. Peters Church	Release	7 acres on Saluda River
Susanah See to Nicholas See	Deed	88 acres on the waters of Saluda
Nicholas See to John Gartman	Deed	90 acres on the waters of Saluda
Peter Lampkin to the Trustee of Sarah Seibels	Bill of Sale	3 negroes--Kate, George & Adam
Thomas Rall to Jonas Matthias	Deed	100 acres on 6 mile Creek
Tobais Jones & Wife to Macajah Martin	Power of attorney	---------------
Gasway Bowen & Wife to Martin Free	Deed	100 acres on Hollow Creek waters
Henry Seibels to John Countz	Sheriffs Titles	80 acres on Crims Creek
John Minick & others to John Countz	Deed	162 3/4 acres on Crims Creek
John D. sharp to James S. Guignard	Deed & plat	2 acres on Broad River
Samuel Kennerly to Benjamin Hart	Deed	474 acres on Saluda
John Rickert & wife to George Barnard Shrum	Lease & Release	50 acres on Jinkins branch waters of Saluda
Prosey Shrum to Denis Gibson	Deed	50 acres on Jinkins branch waters of Saluda
John Snider & wife John Threewits	bill of Sale of 3 negroes	------
Jacob Lucas to Henry Metz	Bill of Sale	------
Adam Metz to J. Henry Metz	Lease & Release	100 acres on the waters of Broad River
Benjamin Hart to Samuel Kennerly	To Bonds & Mortgage	Mortgate for 474 acres of land on Saluda River 2 Bonds for $10,000
Samuel Caver & Wife to Laurence Crim	Lease & Release	100 acres on Beaver Creek
Laurance Crim to Robert Seawright	Deed	100 acres on Beaver Creek

At what time dated	For what consideration	At what time proved And Recorded
1st May 1813(?)	$300	5th June 1817
26 Decr 1812	$250	5 June 1817
15th Feby 1817	$130	Recorded 7 June 1817
12 Augt 1790	Ten shillings	10th June 1817
5th Feby 1814	$100	10th June 1817
14th Febry 1817	$350	10th June 1817
16th June 1808	$848	21st June 1817
26 May 1817	$300	28 June 1817
-------	----	4th Augt 1817
17th Feby 1817	$40	6 Augt 1817
2 Dec 1816	$225	22 Augt 1817
15th March 1817	$800	22 Augt 1817
7 April 1817	----	29th Augt 1817
16 July 1817	$10,000	9th Septr 1817
4th Decr 1795	Ten shillings	19th Septr 1817
10th January 1807	$110	19th Septr 1817
4th Octr 1817	$1200	9 Octr 1817
20th Janry 1817	$300	15 Octr 1817
19 Jany 1791	Ten shillings	15 Octr 1817
16th July 1817	$10,000	18th Octr 1817
30th July 1792	L 30 sterling	22d Octr 1817
28 March 1805	$325	22d Octr 1817

Names of the parties and their additions	What kind of conveyance	Quantity of land and on what water course
John Griffin to Daniel Griffin	Deed	500 on branches of black Creek waters of N Edisto
John Griffin to Daniel Griffin	Deed	1200 acres on the waters of black Creek
Gabriel Frideg to Zacheriah Canty	Deed	31 acres on the Congaree Congaree River
William Kinsler & Anna Kinsler to Zachariah Canty	Deed	400 acres on Congaree Creek
William Kinsler to Zachariah Canty	Deed	136 acres on Six Mile Creek
William Kinsler to Zachariah Canty	Deed	496 acres on Six Mile Creek
Amos Banks to Jacob Lorick	Sheriffs Titles	75 acres on hollingsheds Creek
Mathias Quattlebom to John W Sheely	Deed	200 acres on waters of Saluda
Joseph Burgess to Joshua Burges	Deed of Gift	one Negro boy
Rivers Gunter to John Quattlebom	Deed	921 acres on little black creek
John P. Bond to John Quattlebom	Deed	1394 acres on lightwood Creek
William Hall to John Dent	Deed	676 acres on lightwood Creek waters
Michael Wise to George Rall	Deed	100 acres on Horspen Creek waters of Saluda
John Bush to Solomon Martin	deed	100 acres between Broad & Saluda Rivers
Jacob Erigle to Frances Koon	Deed	41 acres on bear Creek
James H. Taylor to the assigness of Charles Pinckney	Mortgage	471 acres on the Congaree River
David Callaham to Samuel Walker	deed	400 acres on Marlers branch
George Liks to Benjamin Wingard	Deed	378 acres on the head of Congaree Creek
John Gibson to Wiley Bull Bales	Deed	nine acres S. Side of Saluda
Mathias Yonce to Christopher H. Wiggers	Deed	125 acres on branches of the WaterRee Creek
Charles F. Conheim to Samuel Corben	Deed	340 acres on Beaver Creek Conagree Waters
Martin Fouts to Frances Coon	Deed	277 acres on Crooked branch

69

At what time dated	For what consideration	At what time proved And Recorded
21 Octr 1817	$100	23d Octr 1817
1 Octr 1817	$250	23 Octr 1817
5 May 1805	$300	30 Octr 1817
5th May 1805	$400	30th Octr 1817
15 Septr 1804	$136	30 Octr 1817
15th Septr 1804	$490	30th October 1817
3d Novr 1813	$6	4th Novr 1817
25 Novr 1813	$500	10 Novr 1817
5 Augt 1817	Love & affection	11th Novr 1817
31 Decr 1816	$100	11th Novr 1817
1st Feby 1816	$2500	12th Novr 1817
5 Septr 1817	$1000	13 Novr 1817
27 Octr 1817	$300	14th Novr 1817
4th Octr 1817	$500	Novr 14th 1817
5th July 1815	$40	22 Novr 1817
26 March 1817	$16.001(?)	24th Novr 1817
16 Decr 1816	$400	29 Novr 1817
19 Decr 1801	$321	1st Decr 1817
26 Augt 1805	$10	1st Decr 1817
25 Decr 1816	$525	2 Decr 1817
9 Octr 1817	$500	2d Decr 1817
13th Septr 1814	$105	8th Decr 1817

Names of the parties and their additions	What kind of conveyance	Quantity of land and on what water course
William Wingard to Denis Gibson	Deed	100 acres on 16 mile branch waters of Saluda
John Freshley to John Frazer	Deed	78 acres on the Wateree Creek
Samuel Wingard to Jacob Bickley	Deed	87 acres on Saluda
Daniel Wingard to Jacob Bickley	Deed	120 acres on the N. Side of Saluda
Christian Patrick to John Wolfe	Deed	350 acres Congaree
George Setzler to Henry Ruff	Deed	20 acres on Crims Creek Broad River
Margaret Slappy to Randolph Geiger	Power of attorney	

I do hereby Certify that these three sheets of paper annexed contain a correct and true Return of the Deeds and other conveyances Recorded in the office of Register of mesne Conveyance for Lexington District for the year Ending the first of January 1818

John McCreless Regr.

At what time dated	For what consideration	At what time proved and Recorded
Novr 12th 1817	$250	8 Decr 1817
10th Feby 1816	$300	9th Decr 1817
15th Jany 1813	$800	9th Decr 1817
12 July 1813	$1,000	10th Decr 1817
19th Jany 1803	$1,740	17th Decr 1817
4th Feby 1816	$120	24 Decr 1817
27th Octr 1817	---	24th Decr 1817

Agreeable to an Act of the General assembley of the 1785 I have hereby Returned the following memorial of District of Lexington in the office of Register of Mesne State for the year Ending the first day of January 1819.

Names of parties and other additions	What kind of conveyance	Quantity of land and what water course
Stephen Williams to John Black	deed	Sixty nine acres on the waters of Hollow Creek
Mary Hill to John Black	deed	54 acres on the waters of Hollow Creek
Barnet Lybrand to Jacob Taylor	deed	115 acres on Horse Creek waters of Saluda
Regann Schlice to John Lowerman	deed	100 acres on big Johns Creek waters of Saluda
John See to Abraham Harris	deed	150 acres on little creek waters of the congaree
John W. Vanzant to to Mathias Oswalt	deed	95 acres on Hollow Creek waters of Saluda
Susana See to Henry See	deed	72 acres on the waters of Beaver Creek
John Hietle(?) & the heirs of Blackley to George Montz	deed	100 acres on the waters of Congaree Creek
William Lybrand to John Snelgrove	deed	12 acres on Island in Saluda River
David Hoke to John Bouknight Senr	deed	78 acres on hollingsheads Creek
Zacharias Norts to John Bouknight	deed	100 acres on Broad River or the waters thereof
John Baughman to William Geiger	deed	150 acres on South branch waters of the Congaree Creek
John Baughman to William Geiger	deed	602 acres on the waters of the Congaree Creek
John Geiger to James(?) Rogers	a Ret. for money	paid for three acres of land on the Conagree
J. Henry Baughman to William Baughman	deed	75 acres on the Congaree River
Gabriel Clements to John Geiger	deed	100 acres on the Congaree Creek
Jacob Geiger to John Geiger	Lease & Release	2560 acres on the Congaree Creek
Abraham Harris & others to Wm & Harman Geiger	deed	356 acres on the Congaree River
Jacob Snider to Jacob Rall	Deed	146 acres beaverdam Creek Saluda
James Pou to Lewis Pou & Henry Seigels	deed	one acre lot in Granby Village

State of South Carolina passed the 17th day of March
Deeds and other conveyances proved and Recorded in the
Conveyance for said District to the office of Secretary of

At what time dated	For what consideration	At what time Recorded
24th Decr 1816	$207	26 January 1818
20th Decr 1816	$150	26 Jany 1818
18th Decr 1815	$250	26 January 1818
22d July 1814	$250	27th January 1818
14th Octr 1818	$25	27th January 1818
11th Decr 1815	$100	28th January 1818
25th Octr 1808	$50	28th Jany 1818
12th Augt 1816	$37	29 Jany 1818
18th Augt 1817	$188	29th Jany 1818
26 Sept 1816	$40	29 Jany 1818
1st Decr 1816	$100	30th January 1818
3d Jany 1818	$180	7th February 1818
11th Feby 1813	$50	7th Febuary 1818
17th Janry 1817	$75	12th Feby 1818
29th March 1817	$120	12th Feby 1818
L June 1797	₤ 10 sterling	13th Feby 1818
8th Jany 1790	10 shillings	13th Febury 1818
12th Jany 1818	$2100	16 Feby 1818
20th March 1809	$450	19th Feby 1818
18th Decr 1817	$14-0	21st Feby 1818

Names of parties and other additions	What kind of conveyance	Quantity of land and what water course
John Duke to Abraham Geiger	deed	800 acres on Bull Swamp waters of Edisto
John Souter to Michael Lorick	deed	49½ acres in fork of Broad & Saluda Rivers
John Souter to Michael Lorick	deed	34 acres on Saluda River Saluda River
Gasper Souter to John Souter	deed	49½ acres on Saluda River
Gasper Souter to Michael Lorick	deed	52 acres on Saluda River
John Swecard to Michael Lorick	deed	33 acres on Saluda River
George Lorick to Michael Lorick	deed	350 acres on Saluda and the waters thereof
Gasper Souter to John Souter	deed	34 acres on Saluda River
Christopher Sharp to Gasper Souter	deed	49½ acres on Saluda River
Henry M. Rutledge by his attorney to Andrew Tarrer	deed	176 acres on waters of Saluda River
Margaret Hampton to George Eigleberger	deed	246 acres on Broad River
John Drehr & others to Christian Kyzer	deed	100 acres on the waters of Saluda
Henry See to Christian Kyzer	deed	112 acres on Beach Creek waters of Saluda
John Hallman & Michael Beatenbough to Margaret Hallman	deed	two sixths of 100 acres on Broad River waters
Arney Hutchison to John Enlow	deed	one Sixth part of 100 acres waters of Broad River
Charles Bundrick to Spencer Morgan	deed	10 acres between Broad & Saluda Rivers
James Beard & wife to Spencer Moragn	deed	100 acres on the waters of Broad River
Simeon Eleazer to Spencer Morgan	Release	30 acres on Broad River
Simeon Eleazer to Spencer Morgan	Release	10 acres on Broad River
Christian Long & wife to Andrew Holman	Release	100 acres on the waters of Broad River
Benjamin Busby to Henry Kunkle	deed	50 acres on the wateree Creek
Henry Weaver to John Lee	deed	300 acres on a branch of 12 mile Creek

At what time dated	For what consideration	At what time recorded
3 Decr 1817	$150	23d Feby 1818
11th Feby 1817	$350	24th Feby 1818
11 Feby 1817	$450	24th Feby 1818
14 Augt 1816	$100	24 Feby 1818
9 March 1811	$300	25 Feby 1818
9th Sept 1816	$330	25th Feby 1818
8th March 1811	$2,000	25th Feby 1818
14 Augt 1816	$100	25 Feby 1818
20th Decr 1811	$246.25 cts.	26 Feby 1818
11th Feby 1808	$35	27 Feby 1818
26 Novr 1816	2460	5th March 1818
18 Novr 1817	$245	5 March 1818
12 Decr 1815	$225	5 March 1818
27th Decr 1813	no consideration mentioned	9 March 1818
13th Novr 1815	$35	9 March 1818
5 Jany 1801	Ł 5	11 March 1818
13 May 1794	70 Ł sterling	12 March 1818
13 June 1795	15 Ł sterling	13 March 1818
13 June 1795	3 Ł sterling	13 March 1818
26 Decr 1794	10 shillings	14th March 1818
4 April 1806	$200	14 March 1818
16 Octr 1817	$100	16 March 1818

Names of parties and other additions	What kind of conveyance	Quantity of land and what water course
John Oswalt to Michael Wingard	deed	612 acres on a branch of 12 mile Creek
John Lee to Michael Wingard	deed	420 acres on Branches of mile Creek
John Roof to Godfrey Roof	deed	165 acres 12 mile Creek waters of Saluda
Benjamin Roof to Godfrey Roof	deed	50 acres 12 mile Creek waters of Saluda
Frederick Kelly to Joseph Lites	deed	34 acres on bear Creek waters of Saluda
Susana Snider to to William Dent	deed	700 acres Rock Creek waters of Saluda
Mathias Snider to John Snider	Power of attorney	----------
John Hendrix to Thomas K. Poindexter	deed	120 acres on 12 mile branch waters of Saluda
James Dellet Commr. in Equity to Thomas K. Poindexter	deed	100 acres 14 mile branch waters of Saluda
John Benton to Amos Banks	deed	50 acres on Cut log Creek waters of Saluda
Jacob Fullmer to to John Benton	deed	50 acres on Cut log Creek waters of Saluda
Charles Banks to Amos Banks	Deed of Gift	3 negroes Francis, Nane & Andrew
Drusilla Braselman to Henry Muller	deed	704 acres on the Congaree Creek waters of Congaree R
Mathias Wicker to Susana Lyles	deed	167 acres on waters of Saluda
John W. Shealye Senr William Andrew Shealy	Deed of Gift	of a negro
James D. Ervan to John P. and Sarah Franklow	Deed of Gift for life	negro woman & 2 children Hester, Adam & Jacob
Amos Banks Sheriff to Nicholas Ham	deed	480 acres on the Congaree Creek
Amos Banks Sheriff to Nicholas Hane	deed	150 acres on the waters Congaree Creek
Samuel Oswalt to Christian Lightner	deed	100 acres on Horse Creek waters of Saluda
Thomas Fox Junr to Jesse Fox	deed	300 on the Edisto waters
James Boatwright to Jacob Nounamaker	deed	112 acres on Broad River or waters thereof
Jacob Jefcoat & John Hooker to Simon Redman	deed	250 acres on the waters of Edisto River

At what time dated	For what consideration	at what time recorded
29 Octr 1817	$250	16 March 1818
18th Octr 1817	$150	16 March 1818
20 April 1811	no consideration mentioned	17 March 1818
7 Feby 1816	no consideration mentioned	17 March 1818
1st Augt 1816	$480	18 March 1818
5 Feby 1817	$500	18 March 1818
11 Novr 1817	---	18 March 1818
11th Novr 1816	$650	20 March 1818
---1816	$175	20 March 1818
29 Novr 1817	$312.25	21st March 1818
23d Decr 1811	$160	21 March 1818
27 Jany 1818	Love and affection	21 March 1818
9 February 1818	$600	26 March 1818
--------	$820	27 March
28 Novr 1812	Good will	9 April 1818
29 Jany 1818	love & affection	23d April 1818
11th Apl 1818	$35	23 Apl 1818
14th Apl 1818	$100	23d April 1818
27 Jany 1817	$500	23d April 1818
19 March 1818	$125	23d April 1818
5 Septr 1817	$220	24th April 1818
day of 1812	$84	24 April 1818

Names of parties and other additions	What kind of conveyance	Quantity of land and what water course
Henry Lewey to Frederick Ellisor	deed	100 acres on Hollingsheads Creek
John Friday to Nicholas Hane	deed	12 acers on Congaree River
John Hogg to Jacob Turnupseed	deed	126 acres on the wateree Creek Spring Hill
John Hogg to Jacob Turnupseed	deed	40 acres on the wateree Creek Spring Hill
Amos Banks to Jacob Kynard	deed	waters of Saluda
Catharine Oswalt to Jacob Rice	articles of an agreemt.	Rice to maintain her for her property
Abrahm Fullmer to James Dayley	deed	11 3/4 acres on the wateree Creek
Christian Swigart to Jacob Rice	deed	25 acres on the waters of Saluda
George Golden to Jacob Rice	deed	50 acres on the waters of Saluda
Simpson Sawyer to Arthur H. Fort & Ansel Sawyer	deed	625 acres on the waters of Clouds Creek
John Matheson to John W. Lee	deed	200 acres on the waters of Edisto River
George Slappy to Jacob. C. Slappy	deed of Gift	negro Boy named Epram
Mathias Snider to John Snider	deed	140 acres on Rock Creek waters of Saluda
John Snider & other to to Mathias Snider	deed	140 acres on Rock Creek waters of Saluda
Jacob Snider to John Snider	deed	125 acres on the waters of Saluda
David Boozer to Elizabeth Boozer	Bond for $1000	to provide for the sd. Elizabeth
Margaret Younginer & others to Sabastian Younginer	deed	75 acres on or near Broad River
Margaret Zimmerly & others to Sabastian Younginer	deed	33 1/3 acres on Broad River & waters thereof
Jacob Geiger to Jacob Huffman & Sebastian Younginer	deed	13 acres on Broad River & waters thereof
William Harmon to Henry Dominic	deed	300 acres on Saluda River & waters thereof
Amos Banks Sheriff to William Snelgrove	deed	172 acres on Broad River & waters thereof

At what time dated	For what consideration	at what time recorded
2 Feby 1805	$300	24th April 1818
23d Apl 1818	$700	25 April 1818
27 Septr 1816	$1250	3d May 1818
27th Sept 1816	$1250	7 May 1818
4th May 1818	$90	9 May 1818
28 Jany 1818	---	9 May 1818
21 Feby 1818	$17	9 May 1818
13 Feby 1818	$100	11 May 1818
1 Jany 1818	$250	13 May 1818
14th Jany 1817	$300	13 May 1818
8 Augt 1817	$145	14th May 1818
10 Feby 1818	love & affection	29 May 1818
12 Novr 1817	$200	2 June 1818
7 June 1814	$200	2 June 1818
10 Sept 1810	$50	3 June 1810
8 July 1817	---	5 June 1818
3d Septr 1811	$525	9 June 1818
14 Jany 1815	$466	9 June 1818
30 Decr 1816	$80	12 June 1818
2 Feby 1817	$800	13 June 1818
12 Decr 1817	$2	13 June 1818

Names of parties and other additions	What kind of conveyance	Quantity of land and what water course
Elizabeth Kaigler to David Kaigler	deed	10 acres on the Congaree River or near
Elizabeth Kaigler to David Kaigler	deed	60 acres on the Congaree River or near
Elizabeth Kaigler to David Kaigler	deed	200 acres on the Congree River & waters thereof
Elizabeth Kaigler to David Kaigler	deed	200 acres on the Congaree & near
Elizabeth Kaigler to David Kaigler	deed	38 acres on the Congaree River
Elizabeth Kaigler to David Kaigler	deed	41 acres on the Congaree River
David Kaigler to Elizabeth Kaigler	deed	47 acres on the Congaree River
David Kaigler to Elizabeth Kaigler	deed	87 acres on the Congaree River
David Kaigler to Elizabeth Kaigler	deed	200 acres on the Congaree
David Kaigler to Elizabeth Kaigler	deed	185 acres on the Congaree
Henry Oswalt & wife to George Oswalt Junr	deed	136 acres on Beaverdam Creek Saluda
Henry Oswalt & wife to George Oswalt	deed	200 acres on Hollow Creek waters of Saluda
Christian Lightner to Drury Sawyer	deed	100 acres on Hollow Creek waters of Saluda
Amos Banks Sheriff To John W. Lee	deed	237 acres on waters of Saluda River
Micajah Martin, Joel William and Abner Williams to George D. Lester	deed	567 acres on Hollow creek & the waters thereof
John W. Lee to the heirs of Joseph Williams Decd.	deed	2534 acres on Hollow Creek (25 3/4?)
John Hall Senr to John Matheson	deed	200 acres on the waters of Edisto River
Amos Banks Sheff. to William Snelgrove	deed	700 acres on the waters of 12 mile Creek. Saluda
Gasper Souter to Jacob Souter	deed	175 acres on the waters of in the Saluda Fork
James Kennerly to Gasper Souter	deed	260 acres on the waters of Saluda in the Fork
Gasper Souter to to John Matthias	deed	8 acres on the N Side & on Saluda River
Gabriel Fridig to William Kinsler	deed	320 acres on the waters of Congaree Creek

At what time dated	For what consideration	At what time recorded
5 Octr 1817	$20	13 June 1818
5 Octr 1817	$1500	15 June 1818
25 Octr 1817	$1500	15 June 1818
25 Octr 1817	$400	15 June 1818
25 Octr 1817	$2125	16 June 1818
25 Octr 1817	$1000	16 June 1818
25 Octr 1817	$1125	18 June 1818
25 Octr 1817	$2125	18 June 1818
25 Octr 1817	$400	18 June 1818
25 Octr 1817	$370	18 June 1818
19 Novr 1812	$20	19 June 1818
24 March 1818	$200	19 June 1818
27 Jany 1817	$500	3 July 1818
15th Apl 1817	$19.01 cts	3d July 1818
23d May 1818	$1	3d July 1818
23d May 1818	$1	6 July 1818
25 Jany 1817	$100	6 July 1818
6 July 1818	$110	6 July 1818
9 April 1816	$74	11 July 1818
10th Apl 1813	$260	11th July 1818
25 Oct 1817	Ł 20	11 July 1818
15 July 1818	$250	24 July 1818

81

Names of parties and other additions	What kind of conveyance	Quantity of land and what water course
James Dellet to Jesse M. Howel	Commissioenrs Titles	4770 acres on Savannah hunt & waters thereof
Theofilus Wilson to John Snelgrove	deed	50 acres on Saluda and waters thereof
Abraham Geiger Senr agreement with Gasper Souter	bargain for land	150 acres on Redbank Creek
John Souter to Martin Hook Junr.	deed	150 acres on Saluda River
Samuel Leaver to John Souter	deed	60 acres on Saluda River
Robert Duke to Henry Muller	deed	837 acres on the Congaree Creek & waters thereof
Esaias Saylor to William Geiger, Mary Ann Geiger & Henry Muller	Bond for money	-------
Esayas Sayler to the above named parties	mortgage	50 acres on the Congaree River
James Dellet to Randolph Geiger	Commissioners Titles	80 acres on the Congaree River
John Harris & wife to Abraham Geiger	deed	110 acres on dry Creek waters of the Congaree
John Smith to William Daniel	deed	100 acres on Saluda waters
James Watt to John Watt	deed	287 acres on Rocky Creek Saluda waters
John Watt to Jacob Rall	deed	574 acres on the waters of Saluda River
William Seibels to Michael Bouknight	deed	555 acres on the waters Saluda & Broad River
Michael Hentz to to Sarah Bates	deed	159 acres on the Chinquepin branches Edisto waters
John C. Bell to to Henry Muller	mortgage	1 acres of land & House in Grenby Village
Richard Radcliff to William Geiger & Harman Geiger	deed	975 acres on Ceder Creek Edisto Waters
John T. Seibels to John Uriah Coogler	deed	119 acres in the fork Broad and Saluda Rivers
Peter Hendrix to Jacob Lites	deed	85 acres on a brach of Saluda River
Michael Kennemore to John S. Addy	deed	100 acres on title Hollow Creek waters of Saluda
John Black to Geoger Crotwell	deed	123 acres on the waters of Saluda River
William Hendrix to David Hendrix	deed	77 acres on beach Creek waters of Saluda River

83

At what time dated	For what consideration	At what time recorded
24 March 1818	$2025	1 Augt 1818
23d March 1818	$100	3d Augt 1818
7 March 1813	$150	5 Augt 1818
29 Jany 1817	$700	11 Augt 1818
14 Octr 1815	$600	11 Augt 1818
17 June 1818	$50	18 Augt 1818
26 Jany 1818	$3,000	19 Augt 1818
26 Jany 1818	$3,000	24 Augt 1818
3d Augt 1818	$3,270	25 Augt 1818
11 Feby 1813	$75	25 Augt 1818
6 Apl 1818	$350	25 Augt 1818
28 Decr 1816	$1600	29 Augt 1818
1 July 1818	$4,000	31 Augt 1818
10 July 1818	$257.50/100	3d Septr 1818
5 Augt 1818	$700	12 Septr 1818
7 Septr 1818	$500	16 Septr 1818
21 Septr 1818	**$200**	22d Septr 1818
25 Augt 1818	$64.50 cts.	22 Septr 1818
14 Augt 1818	$556	27 Septr 1818
17 January 1818	$362.50/100	7 Octr 1818
12 Feby 1818	$610	8 Octr 1818
3d January 1816	$300	8 Octr 1818

Names of parties and other additions	What kind of conveyance	Quantity of land and what water course
Henry Weaver to David Hendrix	deed	82 acres on a branch of Rocky Creek waters of Saluda
Henry Seibels to John Metz	deed	600 acres in the fork of Saluda and Broad Rivers
Jacob Drafts Senr to Daniel Drafts	deed	67½ acres on Big Saluda River
John A. Amick & wife to John Summer	deed	100 acres on the wateree Creek near Broad River
John N. Senn to Jacob Souter	deed	50 acres on the waters of SAluda River
John N. Senn to Jacob Souter	deed	90 acres on the waters of Saluda
Jesse W. Whray to John Rooks	deed	2 acre lot near Spring hill waters of Broad River
Abner William, Joel Williams and George D. Lester to Micajah Martin	deed	1400 acres on Hollow Creek waters of Saluda
Peter Redman to John Livingston	deed	240 acres on the waters of N. Edisto River
John Hoover to John Levingston Senr	deed	207 acres on the waters of N. Edisto River
WM. & Martha Edins to their three children	deed of Gift	all their property
John Simmerly to Henry T. Crumpton	deed	124 acres in the fork of Broad & Saluda Rivers
Frederick Class to John Wolfe	deed	100 acres on Savanah hunt waters of the Congaree R.
John Tyler to Frederick Class	Conveyance	100 acres on Savana hunt waters of Congaree
Mary Gartman & others to Dennis Hays	deed	200 acres on the waters Saluda River
David Gartman to Mary Gartman	deed	3d part of 200 acres on Hollow Creek waters of Saluda
Philip Hook & wife to John C. Sharp	deed	135 acres in the fork of Broad and Saluda Rivers
Henry Seibels Sheriff to Jeremiah Walker	Sheriffs Titles	400 acres on the waters of N. Edisto River
Henry Seibels Sheriff to James S. Guignard	Bill of Sale	1 negro woman names Silvia & her child Fena
James S. Guignard to John C. Sharp	a quit claim	of the above name negroes
Ann Geiger to Harman & Wm. Geiger	a Relinquishment of her half of Estate	land and negroes
John Miller to Jacob Hoffman	-------	41 acres in the fork of Broad and Saluda Rivers

At what time dated	For what consideration	At what time proved
11 July 1818	$410	8 Octr 1818
26 Septr 1818	$450	12 Octr 1818
28 Feby 1818	$700	19 Octr 1818
27 Decr 1817	Good will & C	22d Octr 1818
--- Octr 1818	$560	23d Octr 1818
3d Octr 1818	$400	23 Octr 1818
4 Octr 1817	$20	23d Octr 1818
24 May 1818	$1	23d Octr 1818
5 Feby 1818	$200	28 Octr 1818
14 Feby 1818	$200	28 Octr 1818
2nd Novr 1818	love & affection	2 Novr 1818
9 Apl 1817	$200	3d Novr 1818
4 Novr 1818	$850	6 Novr 1818
8 Augt 1794	10 shillings	12 Novr 1818
18 April 1817	$2.6.66/100	12 Novr 1818
17 May 1810	$100	12 Novr 1818
24 Apl 1816	five shillings	13 Novr 1818
2 Novr 1816	$7.50	16 Novr 1818
20 Septr 1816	$525	
20 Augt 1818	$1	1818
9 Octr 1818	love & affection	1818
23d Decr 1815	$120	7 Decr 1818

Names of parties and other additions	what kind of conveyance	Quantity of land and what water course
Mathias Wessinger to Jacob Huffman	deed	11 1/9 acres land in the fork of Broad and Saluda
Susana Wessinger & others to Jacob Huffman	deed	4/9th of 100 acres on the waters of Saluda River
John Wessinger & wife to Jacob Huffman	deed	75 acres on the waters of Saluda or broad river
Needham Davis to Jacob Huffman	deed in usual form	7 acres in the fork of Broad & Saluda Rivers
Samuel Fleming to John Drehr	deed	180 acres in the fork of Broad & Saluda River
John Drehr to Andrew Kaigler	deed	198 acres in the fork of Broad and Saluda Rivers

I do hereby certify that these four sheets of paper annexed contain a correct and true Return of the Deeds and other conveyances Recorded in the office of Register of mesne Conveyances for Lexington District for the year Ending the first of January 1819.

John McCreless Register.

At what time dated	For what consideration	At what time Recorded
21 Apl 1818	$34	7 Decr 1818
6 June 1814	$110	7 Decr 1818
28 June 1814	$70	7 Decr 1818
13 Augt 1814	$28	8 Decr 1818
6 July 1816	$850	21 Decr 1818
1 Novr 1816	$850	22 Decr 1818

Agreeable to the requisitions of the Act of the General
Memorial of Deeds and other Conveyances Recorded
year of our Lord one thousand eight hundred and
1821 and ending January 1st 1822 (inclusive)

Names of the parties buying & selling	Where land lies	Number of acres
Gabriel Friday & Wm Kinsar from Emanuel Friday	Orangeburgh Congaree	640
James Brickell from Jas S. Guignard	Broad River Lexington District	400 Plat
Children of G Addy Deed of Gift from --ddy	Dutch Fork	353
George Spignar (alias Hoover) from Heirs of Michl Beninger	Sandy Run	91 2/3
Same from Catharine Berringer(?)	Do	Do
Christian Swygert from George Swygert & wife Deed of Gift	Dutch Fork	200
Amos Banks from Barbara Corley widow	Lot at Lexington C. H.	½
Adam Mayer Esqr from Amos Banks	Do	½
Thomas Rives from Heirs Saml Hollingshed	Dutch fork Hollingshed Creek	Two tracts 200 & 100

N. B. the above is a bond binding the parties concerned to Stand to the
award of arbitrament in Division of Real & Person Estate

Henry Evins from Edwards Brooks	Lexington Dist. waters of Hollow Creek	150
Charles Bell from Henry Evins	Do	Do
Henry Miller (mortgage) from John Taylor of Columbia	Congaree	493 acres
George Kaigler from Margaret & James Kaigler	Do	200
Same from Same	Do	163
Same from Same	Do	100
Barbara Caver from Henry Caver	Lexington	250
John Rankin Jur. from John Rankins Senr	waters of N Edisto	212
James Rankins from John Rankins Senr.	Do	302
William Bartlet from Mary Hartzmetz	Red bank Creek	100

Assembly of the State of South Carolina the following
in the Registers office in Lexington District for the
Twenty one begining from the 21st day of December

Consideration	When Executed	When Proved and Acknow-ledged
$1000	1st day Novr 1820	11th Decr 1820
4000	15 Augt 1820	15th August 1821
100	15th day of May 1815	15th May 1815
91 2/3 (sic)	29th March 1817	29th March 1817
Do	23rd October 1816	23rd Octr 1816
freely	19th Novr 1819	10th Jany 1821
150	30th May 1820	30th May 1820
200	11th Jany 182-	11 Jany 1821
Division to wife(?)	January 12th 1812	18th January 1821
Ten pound sterling money	4th Septr 1798	--------
$145	Do	1st day of Octr 1798
10,000	13th Jany 1812	---------
2000	10th Augt 1820	15th January 1821
490	Do	Do
250	Do	Do
10 cents	22nd Septr 1820	29th Jany 1821
$100	25 Septr 1820	23rd Jany 1821
$100	2nd Octr 1820	23rd January 1821
freely	26th Jany 1821	27th Jany 1821

Names of the parties buying & selling	Where land lies	Number of acres
John Meetze from Amos Banks, Shff	Dutch fork	50
Same from Same	Do	190
Lewis George from Ulrick Beatenback	Wateree Creek	100
Asel Roberts from Absalom Roberts	Hollow creek	100

[columns change here without designation]

Asel Roberts from Executors of Hallman	$91	34 Lexington Holly Creek
Wm. F. Houseal & wife from Jno Countz Carpenter	700	150 D Fork Broad River Lexington
Henry Grubbs from Phillip Grubbs	250	Do 100 Black
Drury Sawyer from A. Banks Shff LD	500	Do Holly Creek waters of Saluda 95 acres
Same from Same	275	150 acres
Henry Muller from Harmon H. Geiger	1200	Sandy Run waters of Congaree River 83½ acres
John Drehr " Samuel Wingard	150	Lexington Dis 186 acres
John Coughman from Andrew Coughman	10	Do 100 do
Same from Henry Taylor Senr	20	105
John Taylor of Columbia from M. A. Warying Marshal	400	on waters of Broad River Tract 500 acres
Same from Randolph Geiger	15,000	Congaree River 464 acres
Stephen Smith from Frances Davis	200	Lexiington waters of Edisto 270 acres
Mary Nicholas (widow) from Thomas Burket	1821 mortgage	D fork Lexington 176 acres
Mrs. Catharine Bates from John P. Bond	471	Head Branches of Edisto River 314 acres
Catharine Bates from John Bates	$600	Lexington waters of N Edisto 440 acres
Samuel Wingard from Lewis Paker (sic)	1000	do 100 acres
Same from Same	$1	Do 424 Do
Same from the Commissioners in Equity as per of Bickley	1900	Highill Creek Saluda 117 acres

Consideration	When Executed	When Proved and Acknowledged
$7	6th Jany 1821	8th feby 1821
28	Do	Do
100	23d Apl 1807	23 Apl 1807
$5	25th Novr 1820	25th Novr 1820

[columns change here without designation]

9th Feby 1821	9th feby 1821	21st feby 1821
6 May 1820	10th Novr 1820	21st February Do
30th Octr 1820	10th feby 1821	5 March 1821
6th Jany 1821	12 March 1821	12 March 1821
10th Feby 1821	12 March 1821	Do
9th Do	1 Do	14th Do
20th Jan 1821	20th Jane 1821	14th Do
13th feby 1813	31st March 1815	14th Do
20th May 1818	18th July 1818	14th Do
3rd May 1817	1st March 1821	14th Do
30th Septr 1821(sic)	10th March 1821	14th Do
3rd Jany 1811	8th Novr 1815	15th Do
29th March 1821	-----	13th April 1821
15th March 1821	22 March 1821	14th April 1821
16th March 1820	22 March 1820	14th Apl 1821
8th May 1818	8th day of May 1818	14th Apl 1821
7th Do	5th June 1819	14th Do
5th Apl 1820	5th Apl 1820	14th Do

Names of the parties buying & selling	Consideration	Where land lies & number of acres
John Quattlebom from John P. Bond mercht.	150	Lexington 100 acres
Same from Thos Deloach	20	Do 16 acres
Same from Burrel Bell	10	Do 34
John Minick from John Sawyer Senr	1000	Do Lick creek waters of Saluda 300 acres
George Minick from John Minick Senr	10	Do 100 acres
Michl Barr from George Minick	400	100 Do
John Wood from John Bell	300	Do 100 do
John Sheally from John Wood	250	Do
C Clifton from A. Banks Shff L D	55	one third part of 300 acres waters of Saluda
David Epting from Luke Manning, John Threat & wife & others heirs of Manning	100	on Island in Saluda River 10 acres
Frederick Kelly from the Heirs of his Father	$1700	Bears creek of Saluda River 100 acres
John Westley Shurs from John Fanning Schoolmaster	Gift	part of a lot of 196 acres Sandy Run Creek of Congaree
Harmon H. Geiger from Randolph Geiger	400	Sandy Run 150 acres
Frederick Kelly from William Dent	1400	Lexington on the Augusta Road 1500 acres
Peter Redman from Emanuel Huffman	200	Lexington 460
Sebastian Younginger from Jacob Geiger	200	200 acres Broad River
William Calk from James Langford	10	S side Saluda River 389
Harman H. Geiger from John Spears	500	½ of 30 acres heirship of of Phillip See
William Geiger Senr from John Litter Surveyor	62	Pond branch Congaree waters 460 acres
David Kaigler from Thos T. Wellesson	2240	Congaree said to be 370 acres
Same from Same	53	Do 818
Same from Same	$306.03 cts	Do 248

Date Executed	Date Proved	Date Recorded
23rd Octr 1807	6th Octr 1808	16th Apl 1821
9th Novr 1807	19th Dec 1807	Do
20th Octr 1807	3rd Nov 1807	17th Do
27th Octr 1812	9th Decr 1812	Do
30 Septr 1815	8th Apl 1816	Do
4th May 1818	30th March 1821	Do
7th Feby 1818	19th Novr 1818	18th Do
8 Feby 1820	2nd Apl 1820	Do
4th Novr 1817	13th May 1818	Do
10th Decr 1814	3 Feby 1820	Do
25 May 1816	1st June 1816	19th Apl 1821
20 Septr 1817	21st Octr 1820	Do
14 Octr 1820	5th Apl 1821	21st Do
16th Septr 1820	16th Septr 1820	21st Do
4th Octr 1819	15 March 1821	21st Apl 1821
9th January 1819	21st June 1819	Do
17th April 1812	7th Apl 1821	Do
3rd Feby 1821	6 April 1821	Do
8th Do	3rd Do	Do
5th March 1821	21st Apl 1821	Do
Do	Do	23 Do
Do	Do	Do

Names of the parties buying & selling	Consideration	Where land lies & number of acres
Same from Same	580	Do 49 acres
Martin Free from George Rall	80	Holly Creek 339 acres
Thos T. Willisson Esqr from David Kaigler	294	Congaree lower Grounds 49 acres [entire above entry stricken]
M. Conheim & G. Scott & Jacob Huffman	Marriage Contract	---------
William Baker Senr from John Haig Blake Charleston	30,000	Congaree Swamp 1719 acres
Henry Seibels from Thos J. Willison Esqr C E C District	2805	Do 335
Benjamin Jefcoat from Conrod Barsh	857	Lexington 1014 acres
Godlip Sox from West Coughman	50	Lexington 244
Catharine Rall from Samuel Weaver	10 shillings	Holly Creek
Drury Sawyer from George Sawyer	$150	Lexington 60
Micajah Martin from Drury Sawyer	1000	2 tracts Holly Creek 1st 2nd 95 acres
Sarah Jackson from Macajah Martin	Do	Do
Lewis Jones from Levi Young	200	160½ acres range North 34 Misoura
Nathan Cook of fairfield from Samuel Richardson	300	Wateree Creek Dutch Fork 100 acres
Same from Thos Boyd Junr	600	378 acres Dutch fork
Absalom Hendrix from Michael Kreps	260	Holly creek 90 acres
Dennis Chupp from Jacob Souter	$600	S side Saluda River Lexington 50 acres
Same from Jacob Chupp	80	Do 403
Same from Mathias Senn	750	Do 50
Same from William Senn	------	Saluda River Senns falls 5 acres
Saml Williams from Stephen Williams	Bill of sale for negros	Lexington
Susanah Lyles from Drucilla Brazilman	820	D fork 410

Date Executed	Date Proved	Date Recorded
Do	Do	Do
22nd Jany 1820	5th Augt 1820	Do
23rd March 1821	23rd March 1821	23 Aprl 1821
	[entire above entry stricken]	
24th Jany 1821		23 Apl 1821
1st March 1821	16th March 1821	25th Apl 1821
16 March 1821	16th March 1821	Do
27th Jany 1820	27th Jany 1821	28th Do
7th day of Jany 1815	7th Jany 1815	5th May 1821
1st Octr 1794	31st Octr 1795	17th Do
19th feby 1821	12th May 1821	19th Do
31st March 1821	23d May 1821	23rd May 1821
1st May 1821	23rd May 1821	Do
9th Apl 1821	25th May 1821	2nd June 1821
28th Augt 1817	28th Augt 1817	7th Do
17th March 1820	23rd March 1820	Do
9th June 1821		11th Do
22 Decr 1820	13th January 1821	23rd June 1821
13th January 1821	Do	Do
Do	19th Augt 1821	Do
Do	30th Jany 1821	Do
25th feby	22nd June 1821	25th June 1821
28th July 1818	12 June 1821	27th June

Names of the parties buying & selling	Consideration	Where land lies & number of acres
Andrew W. Shealy from Matthias Quattlebom	2000	in said Dist. on Augusta Road 328
A. H. Fort from Daniel Rambo	400	2 tracts 1000 acres Black Creek
John Coogle from William Burgess	500	Black Creek 200
Same from Same	5	Do 11½ acres
Daniel Huffman from Peter Redman	425	430 acres High hill branch
West Coughman from Christopher Coughman	500	Twelve mile Creek several tracts in all 730 acres
Same from Emanuel Corley	50	Do 50
John Bates from Michael Kinard	600	450 acres Lexington
West Coughman from Emanuel Corley	100	124 acres on Twelve mile Creek
John W. Lee from Amos Banks Shff L D	111	200 on Charleston road Davis place
West Coughman from Martin Lybrand	66	Saluda waters 225 acres
Alexr. Jenkins from James & Sarah Hendrix	$100 mortgage	N side of Saluda 165 acres
Henry Hendrix from Jacob Rall	42	240 acres Beaver Dam Creek
Same from George Snider	740	Do 106
George Lorick from Samuel Kennerly & Abner Blocker	3,300	Saluda 456 acres
Jesse Fox from Thomas Fox Jr	600	½ of 640 Chinquepin N Edisto
The Commissioners in Equity C. B. Heirs of Blake to David Kaigler	326.3 & 3/4	Lexington said to be 68 3/4 acres
Same from Same	224	Do 49
Same from Same	3240..87½	Do 307
Same from Same	13986	Do 118
Dennis Hays from Peter Shumpard	100	Edgefield Dist. 644 acres
Jacob Rall from A. Banks Sheriff	16	Lexington Dist. 100

Date Executed	Date Proved	Date Recorded
10th March 1821	25th June 1821	29th June
3rd Jany 1821	28th June 1821	29th June
14 July 1821	18th July 1821	18th July
Do	Do	Do
2nd May 1820	3rd May 1820	20th Do
18th Feby 1811	26 April 1813	21st Do
16th day of 1816 (sic)	4th July 1821	27th Do
15th Feby 1820	23rd March 1821	28th Do
16th Novr 1816	4th July 1821	1st Augt 1821
10th Feby 1821	21st Do	2nd Do
7th May 1817	7th May 1817	Do
27th Octr 1818	6th Augt 1821	7th Augt 1821
20th July 1820	6th Augt 1821	Do
17th July 1821	6th Do	Do
10 Novr 1820	23rd July 1821	8th Do
26th May 1821	4th June 1821	Do
5th March 1821	1st Augt 1821	Do
Do	Do	9th Do
Do	Do	10th Do
Do	Do	Do
20 June 1821	9th Augt 1821	13th Do
9th Decr 1820	9th Decr 1820	13th Do

Names of the parties buying & selling	Consideration	Where land lies & number of acres
William Senn from David Senn	40	Six mile Creek 25 acres
Nathan Cook from John Meetze	150	waters of Broad River 2 tracts 240 acres
David Kyzer from Sarah Taylor	50	Lexington District 1000 acres Congaree Creek
Daniel Lomanack from Christopher Satzer & others	50	Holly Creek waters of Saluda 50 acres
George Addy to his children	Gift	Broad River 64 acres
John Friday in trust for his children from Jacob Rumph	£ 5	Fridays Mill Creek 100
Michael Oswalt from Jacob Hallman	$43	100 acres waters of twelve mile Creek
Samuel Oswalt from Michael Oswalt	40	Do
Michael Wingard from Samuel Oswalt	40	Do
Michael Wingard from Samuel Wingard	300	180 acres High Hill Creek
John Shuler from the Executors Christian Wingard	20	15 acres waters of Saluda
Same from Thomas Shuler	2500	219 acres Saluda
George Leaphart from William Wilson	100	41 acres S side Saluda River
Frederick Shaffer from Henry Hare of Tennessee	321	100 acres Camping Creek
Jacob Mayer from William Hartman & wife	150	136 acres Stephens fork
George Mayer from Joseph Baker & wife	340	136 acres on Stephens Creek
The wife of Jacob Mayer from John Henry Wearts	Gift	150 acres Edgefield District Big Creek
Catharine Gartman Junr. from Honorius Riddle	200	Big Holly Creek 66 acres
John William Fulmer from John Batey	£ 30	90 acres Beach Creek
Henry See from Sheriff Partition of Anasticca Fulmer	$71	Saluda waters 90 acres
Catharine Gartman from Christian Kyzer	400	do 112 acres
John C. Martin from Henry Grubbs	100	N side of Black Creek 100 acres
Samuel Archer from Joshua Wingard	400	18 mile branch waters of Saluda 100 acres

Date Executed	Date Proved	Date Recorded
2nd June 1821	14 July 1821	14th Do
13th Do	15th Augt 1821	16th Do
8th Novr 1818	4th May 1819	11 Septr 1821
22nd June 1816	13th Augt 1819	Do
8th Septr 1821	8th Septr 1821	12th Do
21st December 1793	6th May 1794	22nd Septr 1821
13th Jany 1818	14th Jany 1818	25th Do
11th Novr 1820	17th Septr 1821	Do
15th Septr 1821	17th Septr 1821	Do
24th Feby 1819	5th July 1819	Do
5th Septr 1821	14th Septr 1821	2nd Octr 1821
9 March 1821	9 March 1821	Do
24th Sept 1821	24th Septr 1821	Do
29th Novr 1819	11 Dec 1820	3 Do
12th Decr 1814	4th March 1815	Do
20th Do 1820	29th Decr 1820	Do
15 Septr 1821	15th Septr 1821	Do
3rd Decr 1819	6th May 1820	13th Octr 1821
23th Novr 1794	24th Novr 1794	Do
13th Septr 1814	----	13th Octr 1821
15th March 1821	5 Apl 1821	Do
24th July 1821	17th Octr 1821	Do
1st May 1817	1st May 1817	19th Do

Names of the parties buying & selling	Consideration	Where land lies & number of acres
Same from William Wingard	500	Head of Congaree Creek 228 acres
James Cayce from A. Banks Sheriff L D	11	Granby forks of Harks & Kennerlys Road 2 acres lot
Amos Banks from Daniel Rambo Exr of Laurence Rambo	600	3 Tracts 100 acres each on Black Creek 3000
Sion Waters (Marlborough) from Susanah Hall	20	Lexington 16 acres
John H. High from John Younginger	200	60 acres on Saluda waters in the fork
John W. Lee or Sion Waters George Haltiwanger Sheriff	33.98	one 1/3 part of five hundred acres Lexington District
David Derick from James S. Guignard (Columbia)	45	45 acres on Bookmans Creek Lexington D Fork
Nicholas House from Benjamin Sturkie	65	$36
Micajah Martin from Drury Sawyer	900	102½ acres on Holly Creek
Jane Redman mortgage from Peter Redman	120.66	68 acres Lexington
James Cayce from G. Haltiwanger Sheriff	50	1 acres in Granby Lexington
Drury Bowland from James H. Mellard	50	100 acres Pond on Bea hunters branch
William Chapman from John Chapman (newberry)	110	142 acres on Wateree Creek Lexington
John Chapman from Henry Cunkle	200	200 acres
Barbara Corley from Thos T. Willisson (partition)	20	1 3/4 acres on the road Twelve Creek Lexington
Christian Gable from Jacob Risinger (Edgefield)	75	20 acres Holly Creek Lexington
Same from John C. Martin	300	60 acres Do
Heirs of Michael Kreps from John Meetze Bond	300	a Described Tract by Sale from Sheriff to Grantor
Catharine Gartman from Michael Eragle	350	67 acres on Holly Creek
Michael Eragle from George Carnlin	300	67 acres Do
George Carline from Lewis Carline	50	67 acres Do
Jacob Drafts from the Heirs of Christopher Coughman deceased	250	Little horse creek 160

Date Executed	Date Proved	Date Recorded
18 July 1821	18th July 1821	24th Do
12th Augt 1820	22nd Octr 1821	25th Do
3rd January 1821	14th Novr 1821	29th Novr 1821
29th Septr 1820	31st Oct 1821	9th Novr Do
27th June 1821	30st Octr 1821	Do
7th Apl 1821	31 Octr 1821	10th Do
5th Dec. 1820 (sic)	22 May 1820	Do
7th Octr 1809	9th Octr 1809	Do
31st March 1821	12 May 1821	14th Do
14 March 1821	15th Jany 1821	19 Do
19th Octr 1821	12 Novr 1821	Do
6th Jany 1821	29 May 1821	20 Novr 1821
24 Apl 1817	24 Apl 1817	Do
25 January 1817	20 January 1817	Do
1st Nov 1820	20 Nov 1821	Do
3rd January 1818	28th Augt 1818	22nd Do
25 Augt 1818	12th March 1819	23rd Do
25 Octr 1821	23rd Nov 1821	Do
18th Augt 1821	31st of ------	Do
1st Novr 1818	17 Novr 1819	Do
15 Octr 1813	12 Octr 1816	Do
28 Jany 1815	19th March 1821	

Names of the parties buying & selling	consideration	Where land lies & number of acres
Henry Milar from Wm Bartlet & mother	200	55 acres Lexington
William Wilson from Henry Miller	60	62 acres Do
William Kinsler from Nicholas Ham	650	260 acres on Beards branch waters of Saluda

[columns change here without designation]

Asel Roberts from Executor of Hallman	Lexington Holly Creek	$91
Wm F. Houseal from John Countz Carpenter	D B river	700
Henry Grubbs from Philip Grubbs	Lexington B Creek	250
Henry Muller from John T. Seibels mortgage of negroes	Do	1821
David Weaver from Nicholas vansant Deed	Do	300
Drury Sawyer from Amos Banks Sheriff	Do	

Date Executed	Date Proved	Date Recorded
18th Decr 1819	19 January 1820	29 Do
10th Novr 1821	10 Novr 1821	Do
25th Novr 1821	13 Decr 1821	15th Decr 1821

[columns change here without designation]

9th February 1821   21st feby 1821

10th November 1820   Do

10 Feby 1821   5 March 1821

1st March 1821   Do

2nd August 1814   12 March 1821

Memorial of Deeds & other instruments Registered in Lexington District in the year of 1821.

Agreeable to an Act of the General Assembly passed
our Lord one thousand Seven Hundred and Eighty five
and other conveyances proved and recorded in the office
for the year ending January first 1820.

Names of Parties	What kind of conveyance	Number of acres on what water course
Henry Weaver to John Withers	Deed	271 acres on-----
John W. Lee to Sarah Jones	Do	237 acres on the cross leading from Columbia
Barbara Corley to the commissioners of Public Buildings	do	2 acres on the Road lead- to Augusta
Thos Hamton to Nicholas Hane	Do	460 acres Congaree River in Lexington & Richland
Henry Roof, Eliz Rodd, Margret Mayor, Solomon Sligh, Geo Eigleberger, Katharine Eigleberger to William Summers	Do	23 acres on a branch of beaver Creek waters Saluda
The Same to the Same	do	53 acres on Watree Creek
Taylor of the Town of Columbia to Elisha Daniel & John McCreless	do	498 acres on Congaree River
Susanah Hall to John Swinney	do	10 acres
(preceding repeated)		
Levi Richardson, Rhoda Richardson, Solomon Richardson, to James Richardson	Deed	280 acres a Small part in Edgefield District
William Taylor to Aberhart Holman	do	16 acres on Hell hole Creek
Ruth Taylor to the same	do	10 acres on do
Celia Taylor to the same	do	16 acres on do
Sarah Taylor to the same	do	16 acres on do
John Wing to the same	do	16 acres on do
William Bloodworth to the same	do	16 acres on do
Richard Waters to the same	do	16 acres on do
Elizabeth Taylor to Margaret Singly	Gift do	25 acres on Holly Creek
Amos Banks to Elizabeth Oswalt	Deed	631 acres on Holly Creek
Henry Roof to John Roof	do	234 acres on Twelve Mile Creek

the Eighteenth day of March in the Year of
I herewith Transmit the following Memorial of Deeds
of Registry of Mense(sic) Conveyance for Lexington District

Consideration	When Executed	When proved & acknowledged
$500	25th Nov 1819	30th Nov 1819
$72	Sept 8 1819	Jany 12, 1820
$100	24th Jany 1820	Feby 24th 1820
12000	Nov 2rd 1819	Jany 5th 1820
111.25	Jany 5th 1820	Jany 8th 1820
106	5th day Jan 1820	8th Jany 1820
5000	8th Decr 1819	11th Feb 1820
22	8th Jany 1819	20th March 1819
(preceding repeated)		
500	19th July 1817	29th July 1817
32	5th Decr 1818	23rd March 1820
21	Do	Do
30	Do	Do
32	Do	Do
32	Do	Do
32	Do	Do
32	Do	Do
---------	July 29th 1819	July 29th 1819
100	21st day February 1820	Feb 21st 1820
300	5th March 1818	------------

Names of Parties	What kind of conveyance	Number of acres on what water course
William Wingard to John Eddins	Do	130 acres
Jonathan Taylor to the Same	do	16 acres
Mark Lott Senr to Mark Lott Junr	Do	368 acres on Lightwood Creek waters of N Edisto
Mark Lott to William Livingston	Deed	368 acres on Lightwood Creek
William Livingston to Abraham Barton	Do	part of the same land
Abraham Barton to David Callaham	do	the same land
Frances Davis to David Callaham	Do	243 acres Southside of the Long arm of Marlers branch
Isham Langley to David Callaham	Do	40 acres on Chinquepin Creek
John W. Lee to Micajah Martin	Do	200 acres on Lightwood Creek
The same to the same	Do	150 acres on Malers(sic) branch
The Court of Equity to Henry Muller	Title	500 acres Congaree River sold to make partition of the heirs of Haugabook
The same to make partition of the Heirs of Andrew Kailer(sic) to James Kaigler	Do	50 acres
Levi Haugabook to John Haugabook	mortgage	100 acres Haugabook Swamp
Michael Oswalt Jr. to Jacob Rall	Deed	10 acres beaver Creek Lexington Dist.
Amos Banks to Frances Koon	Titles	300 acres on bear Creek sold to make a Division among the heirs of George Long
Henry Gaulman to John P. Bond	Deed	100 acres Lightwood Creek waters of N Edisto River
Samuel Fleming of Edgefield to John W. Lee	Deed	200 acres on west Creek Edgefield District
Daniel Boatright to Samuel Fleming	do	332 acres on Lightwood Creek
John Lipps to Christian Wingard	do	90 acres Lexington Dist.
Christian Rall & Nancy Rall to William Dent	do	134 acres waters of big Saluday River
Jeremiah Edwards to George Stidham	do	50 acres on Black Creek

Consideration	When Executed	When proved & acknowledged
100	15 Jany 1818	24 Feby 1818
12½	28th Decr 1818	5 April 1820
150	14th Decr 1803	28th February 1804
$400	2nd December 1805	5th April 1820
400	9th June 1810	August 15th 1810
400	15th March 1812	1st September 1816
100	14th Septr 1813	2rd April 1820
20	18th March 1815	21st Octr 1815
400	10th March 1820	7th April 1820
100	10th March 1820	7th April 1820
805	1st Nov 1819	15th April 1820
---	17th Septr 1819	5th April 1819(sic)
150	1st January 1820	21st April 1820
20	26th Nov 1812	25th December 1812
250	1st day of May 1820	1st May 1820
100	20th April 1820	20th April 1820
$1000	16th Decr 1819	4th May 1820
130	23rd July 1819	16th November 1819
125	26th December 1818	26th December 1818
1000	2nd March 1820	2nd March 1820
100	19th March 1819	21st August 1819

Names of Parties	What Kind of conveyance	Number of acres on what water course
Samuel Bloodworth to Benjamin Coffill	do	100 acres on a small creek of Chinquepin
Henry Weaver to Jacob Kammoner	Do	1912 acres on Twelve mile creek
Jacob Hall to Miner Woolley	Do	30 acres on waters of N Edisto River
John Hall to Jacob Hall	Do	30 acres on Rocky Branch
William Hall to Miner Woolley	Do	212 acres on a Branch called hogpen
John Hall to Harlley Hollman	Do	100 acres on Rockey Creek waters of N Edisto River
Harlley Holman to Miner Woolley	Do	990 acres on Pockey Creek waters of N Edisto River
Miner Woolley to Zedekiah Watkins	Do	Several tracts 412 acres on Rockey Creek waters of N Edisto
Barbara Corley to Frances Polock	Deed	on half acre lot at Lexington Court House
Gabriel Friday to David Leech	Do	94 acres Long Branch plat of the same
George Wise to John Murph	Do	50 acres in Lexington District
Henry Kyzer to Christian Kyzer	Do	78 acres on Holly Creek
Henry Kyzer to Christian Kyzer	Do	100 acres on waters of Big Hilly Creek
The same to the same	Do	150 acres do
Jacob Drafts to Elizabeth Surgener	Do	19¾ acres on the Road leading from Columbia to Augusta
Peter Mickler, Jacob Mickler, Margaret Younginger, Daniel Mickler & Andrew Mickler to Anna Maria Sivley Beard	do	71½ acres in the fork of B & S Rivers Lexington District Platt
John B. Turnipseed & wf A M S Turnipseed to John C. Sharp	do	71½ acres ditto
James Brickell to James S. Guignard	?? or mortgage	400 acres Lexington Broad River
Henry Weaver (miller) to to Michael Oswalt	Deed	118 acres Twelve mile Creek
Michael Oswalt to Honorius Riddle	Do	118 acres ditto
Benjamin Atkins to D. Ragin and through several persons untill Thomas Warren Senr of Edgefield	Bond to Execute titles when obtained the Right from another who	150 acres on the head of Chinquepin Orangeburgh District decd before Titles made

109

Consideration	When Executed	When proved and acknowledged
50	27th Dec 1813	14th August 1816
2000	4th December 1819	6th April 1820
50	15th January 1818	4th May 1818
50	20th May 1817	---------
260	19th July 1816	4th May 1818
170	12th Nov 1818	22 february 1819
170	17th Nov 1818	16th July 1820
800	25th Feby 1820	31st May 1820
$150	30th May 1820	30th May 1820
50	4th March 1820	4th March 1820
300	23rd January 1819	23 January 1819
200	20th Octr 1819	16th June 1820
400	20th Octr 1819	16th June 1820
200	27th Nov 1819	16th June 1820
96	15th May 1820	15th May 1820
143	5th February 1811	14th Feby 1811
300	25th feb 1820	4th March 1820
1250	15th Augt 1820	15th August 1820
100	11th Nov 1816	15th April 1817
$150	22nd Septr 1819	9th Septr 1820
--	16th Nov 1804	---------------

Names of Parties	What Kind of conveyance	Number of acres on what water course
Amos Banks Esqr to John H. Eiffert	Sheriffs title	1 3/4 acres on the Road to Charleston sold the property of H. Weaver
Nathaniel Corley to R. H. Brumby	Deed from him & heirs only	So much of a tract of land as may be taken by an older survey of Vanderhorst on Lightwood creek N Edisto
Frederick Beard to John Lipps	Deed	200 acres on the 16 mile branch
John Lipp to Dennis Gibson	do	the same Land
Samuel Hoke to Saml Bookman	Do	29 acres on waters of Broad River Lexington
George Bone to the same	Do	95 acres waters Hollingshades Creek waters of Broad River
Jacob Koon and wife Barbara to Saml Bookman	Do	75 acres on Hollingshades Creek
Thomas Shepperd to Saml Bookman	Do	183 acres on Hollingsheds Creek B River
James S. Guignard to Samuel Bookman	Do	47 acres in the fork of B & S Rivers Platt of the same
Whitfield Brooks Esqr Comr in in Equity to Thomas Shepperd	Titles sold for Divr	83 acres in Lexington
Wm Hendrix to John Kyzer	deed	84 acres on Beach Creek plat of the same
George Fetner) RD to John Gill)OD	do	100 acres waters of Saluda River Plat of the same
John Gill to Michael Kreps	Deed	100 acres on the Eighteen mile branch
Henry Kyzer to Michael Kreps	Do	100 acres plat
The same to the same	Do	90 acres on Hollow Creek plat
Jesse Geiger & Une(?) Geiger to Drury Davis	Do	120 acres waters of Saluda River
John Campbell (Edged) to Lewis Jones	Do	160 acres NW Section Illinois Territory
Ruth Taylor to Andrew Hollman	Do	86 acres on
Godfrey Oswalt to Andrew Hollman	Do	70 acres hilhole Creek
Andrew Hollman to John Hollman	Do	70 acres as above

111

Consideration	When Executed	When proved and acknowledged
$2	14 August 1820	
100	22nd Septr 1820	--------
100	8th December 1807	4th Decr 1818
---	26 Decr 1818	26th Decr 1818
130	1st June 1811	21st June 1811
330	20th January 1818	12th June 1818 witness name not signed
600	8th November 1819	26th Nov 1819
1200	first day of June 1820	1st June 1820
35½	2nd July 1820	22nd July 1820
----	Blank	1820
588	26th July 1819	16th June 1820
60	6th March 1805	5th December 1817
160	23rd April 1807	12th Septr 1811
200	16th day of October 1818	24 Septr 1819
200	16 Octr 1818	24 Septr 1819
	7th February 1820	14 Octr 1820
160	16th August 1819	25th October 1819
129	14th Feby 1818	13th Nov 1820
200	10th Decr 1814	11th March 1815
100	14th Feby 1818	1st Nov 1820

Names of Parties	What Kind of conveyance	Number of acres on what water course
Adam Amick to Adam Amick Junr	Do	70 acres on Camping Creek Dutch fork plat
Susanah Hutchison alias Holman to Benedict Mayer	Renunciation of claim	her part of 100 acres on Grims Creek
Frederick Swettenburg to Jacob Countz	Deed	58 acres Dutch fork Grims Creek
Eve M Mayer to Jacob Countz	Do	49 acres Grims Creek D Fork
Wm F. Houseal & wife to Jacob Countz	Do	6¾ acres Dutch fork
Michael Oswalt & Susan his wife to William Dent	Deed	225 acres waters of 12 mile Creek
Henry & Samuel Weaver(?) to the same	do	585 acres do
Samuel Weaver to the same	do	515 acres do
Lewis Dishazo to Micajah Johnston	Lease & Release	260 acres waters of holly creek
Isaiah and Joel Johnston	Deed of Division	of the above land of their Fathers
Amos Banks Esqr to George Price	partition	100 acres Holly creek lands of the Heirs of H. Oswalt
Gab Friday & wife to to William Kinsler & Abm Geiger	Title	606 acres on the Oconee River Georgia Division of John Kinslers lands
Henry M Rutledge by his att. James S. Guignard to R. H. Waring	Deed	72 acres near beards Shoals on Saluda
The same to Gabriel Friday	Do	the above land
Godfrey Earhart to Daniel Earhart	deed of gift	100 acres Saluda
Godfrey Earhart to John Earhart	do	Do

113

Consideration	When Executed	When proved and acknowledged
100	28th January 1818	28th January 1818
----	15th Octr	--------
1800	31st July 1820	30 Octr 1820
600	23rd Octr 1820	23 October 1820
301	31st Augt 1820	30 Octr 1820
$112	23 Septr 1819	2nd Nov 1820
400	14 1818	--------------
500	2nd Nov 1818	15th Septr 1820
₤ 50	25 January 1796	23rd Jany 1797
-----	11th Nov 1820	25th Nov 1820
$396	4th December 1820	4th December 1820
500	1st Nov 1820	Blank
1800	26th Sept 1815	Blank
300	10th July 1817	23 Augt 1817
----	2nd Septr 1817	10th March 1817
-----	Do	Do

Agreeable to the Act of the General Assembly of the State of South
Conveyance Prove(sic) and Recorded in the registers office in Lexington
Ending January Eight(?) 1820

Names of Parties	What kind of conveyance	Consideration
Godfrey Harman to George Younginger	Deed	$250
Abraham Geiger to Thomas Derrick	do	34
Friday Arthur to Claiborne Clifton	do	3000
Thomas T. Willison Esqr Comr in Equity to John Patton	Titles	1840
Jacob Wessinger Junr to Jacob Huffman	Deed	32.61
Elisha Daniel to John Patton	do	200
Amos Banks Esqr to James Cayce	Sheriff Title	180
Randolph Geiger to John Taylor	deed	365
John F. Bamberg to John Drehr	do	140
Martin Witt to Thomas Chargill	do	100
Thomas Chargill to Thomas Warren	do	100
Andrew Kegler to Thomas Taylor Senr	do	℔ 1000
Thomas Taylor Senr to William & Henry P. Taylor	Deed of Gift	-----
James Boatwright to Christian Hankle	Deed of convyce	5000
James Dellet Esqr C E to Peter Chumperd [Schumpert]	Title from the court	805
Jacob Bowers to William Baker	Deed	$700
Jacob Boozer h. C., Wm Boozer Senr, Joseph Strother & Elizabeth Boozer Senr. to Henry Boozer pl.	Deed	1000
William See Plr to David Boozer do	Do	300
Henry Williams Saluda to David Boozer H C	Do	100
Michael Wise to John Boughman	Do	200

Carolina and passed the 17th March 1785 The following memorial of Deeds &
District are returned to the office of Secretayr of State for the Year

Quantity & where	When Executed	What time Proved & Acknowledged
118 acres S side Saluda	8th November 1817	8th November 1817
23 acres Twelve Mile Creek	29th Aprl 1814	23rd May 1814
2852 acres waters of Congaree Creek	9th Feby 1815(8?)	4th January 1819
Several Tracts in several District in Abbeville & Laurens	21st Decr 1818	1st January 1819
100 acres Saluda waters	30th Sept 1816	21st Jany 1819
1081 acres in several pieces & places	16th Nov 1818	10 Decr 1818
100 acres more or less	13 January 1819	25th Jany 1819
9 acres on Congaree River	19th Jany 1819	29th January 1819
150 acres Bear Creek waters of Saluda	20 Decr 1816	17th December 1818
90 acres waters N Edisto	25th June 1808	25 February 1809
98 acres on waters of Chinquepin	18th Jany 1809	10th day of March 1809
420 acres Orangeburgh Big Bull Swamp	9th January 1806	9th January 1806
1019 acres Lexington & Richland Congaree Bull Swamp	24 February 1819	24th Feby 1819
260 acres fork Broad & Saluda Rivers	30 April 1818	30th April 1818
150 acres Holly Creek	3d Augt 1818	5th February 1819
100 acres on Beaver Creek	18th Novr 1818	6th February 1819
196 acres on little rocky creek	21 January 1815	23rd January 1819
199 acres South side Saluda River	25th Augt 1818	13 October 1818
100 acres S side Saluda	28th Novr 1818	11th January 1819
200 acres on Scouters Creek	29th Nov 1814	17th June 1815

Names of Parties	What kind of Conveyance	Consideration
John Horsey to Jeremiah Edwards pl.	do	200
Thomas Wingard to John See	Do	200
John W Sheally to Andrew Shelly	do	500
Jacob & Elizabeth Oswalt to George Oswalt	do	200
John Snider to Frederick Leits	do	450
William Dent to John Snider	do	10
David Waver senr to Micajah Martin	do	200
Martin Free & Elizabeth Free to George Oswalt	do	100
Jacob Bickly to George Derrick	deed	200
Jacob Kelly to John Derrick, Thomas Derrick & Andrew "	do	℔ 500
Jasper Frazier to John Derick	do	100
Thomas Derick & wife to Andrew Derick & John Derick	Lease & Release	℔ 50
John Bell to John Black	deed	$500
Michel Keller to George Fikes	do	℔ 15
Adam Taylor to George Fikes	do	$200
Adam Black to George Fike	do	12
Jacob Lamonack to George Fike	do	45
John Taylor to Michael Taylor	do	50
Adam Black to Martin Fikes	do	400
Gregory Clark to Joseph Lybrand	do	200
Parker Clark to David Shols (Shots?)	do	200
David Shots to Joseph Lybrand	Deed	$400
Andrew Derick & Wife to John Derick	Lease & release	200

Quantity & where	When Executed	What time Proved & Acknowledged
50 acres Big Black Creek	20 Septr 1814	20 Septr 1814
100 acres on waters of Saluda its S Side	21 Feby 1803	24th Septr 1805
200 acres on waters of Saluda called Big Branch	18th March 1819	24 March 1819
100 acres on waters of Big Holly Creek	No month 1818	11th March 1819
118 acres Rocky Creek	6th Jany 1819	18th January 1819
43 acres on the Sd Rocky Creek	6th June 1818	27th June 1818
600 acres on Black Creek N Edisto wtrs	29 May 1818	12th Octr 1819
140 acres waters of Saluda	6th Sept 1818	11 March 1819
80 acres	7th Nov 1817	7 Nov 1817
62 acres	6th May 1797	26 May 1797
36 acres in the fork of B & Saluda	13th Nov 1812	30th Nov 1812
100 acres	24th May 1800	24 May 1800
203 acres waters of Holly Creek	19th Augt 1818	12th Octr 1818
100 acres Holly Creek	6th September 1796	27th Decr 1804
200 acres waters of Big Horse & Twelve Creek	2nd January 1814	11 January 1814
10 acres	20 December 1804	27 Dcr 1804
29 acres Holly Creek	19th Decr 1804	27th Decr 1804
50 acres Horse Creek	27th Sptr 1806	27th Septr 1806
96 acres Holly Creek	12th Septr 1818	12th Sept 1818
150 acres waters of Turkey Creek	23 Septr 1818	23rd Sept
788 acres on S side Bank C	10th Nov 1817	23rd Septr 1818
788 acres on Red bank Creek	23rd Septr 1818	23rd Septr 1818
2 Diferent tracts congt. 105½ acres	30th March 1816	25 April 1816

Names of Parties	What kind of conveyance	Consideration
James Boyd Blacksmith of Ga. to John Derick S. C.	Deed quit claim	30
Thomas T Willison Esqr C E Successor to James Dellet to John Patton	Title by partition	200
The Same to The same	do	------
The same to the same	do	----
The same to John C. Bell	do	5925
[entire above entry stricken]		
Thomas T. Willison Esqr Commissioners in Equity to Amos Banks	do	27
The Same to the same	do	100
William & Elizabeth Houseal to Henry Ruff	Deed	20
John C. Sharp Senr to to Samuel Huffman	do	368.75
James Dellet Esqr C E to John Lorick	Title in Partition	1250
The same to John Countz	do	4355
William Seibels to Henry Seibels	Deed	1000
[entire above entry stricken]		
H. S. Pool to Abraham Geiger	deed	350
John C.Bell to Abraham Geiger	do	300
Eve Boughman to Abm Geiger	do	1000
Harmon Boughman to the same	do	550
A B Stark to the same	do	400
John McCreless to John T. Seibels	do	400
James Dellet C E to Sarah Seibels	Title by the court of Equity	-----
Dyonisuis Blakely to Jacob Haugabook	deed	150
Samuel Jumper pl. To Harmon H. Geiger plr.	do	700
Nicholas Hane to Abm Geiger	do	80

119

Quantity & where	When Executed	What time Proved & Acknowledged
260 acres waters of Broad River Dutch F.	15th January 1815	15th January 1815
one acre a Lot in Granby Congaree	28th Jany 1819	2nd April 1819
700 acres on the North Edisto River	do	do
525 1/3 acres in Saxegotha Township	do	do
for negroes sold [above stricken]		
146 acres on waters of Holly Creek & Clouds Creek	5th April 1819	8th April 1819
300 acres	5th April 1819	do
2 acres	3rd April 1816	3rd April 1816
73 3/4 acres fork of Broad & Saluda Rivers	5th Septr 1818	5th Septr 1818
200 acres on Broad River	5th Augt 1816	4th January 1817
82 acres on waters of Broad River	6th April 1818	8th February 1819
704 acres	2nd March 1818	18th September 1818
640 acres on Congaree Creek	14th Octr 1817	18th September 1818
75 acres	8th Octr 1814	31st Nov 1814
60 acres	6th Feby 1808	---------
200 in 2 several tracts Red bank creek	4th Nov 1811	18th Septr 1818
100 acres waters of Congaree	23rd Decr 1817	18th May 1818
------	9th July 1818	24th May 1819
500 acres Congaree Creek	23 February 1811	23 April 1819
83½ acres Sandy Run	6th May 1819	22nd July 1819
80 acres on the waters of Bull Swamp	31st May 1819	30 July 1809 (sic)

Names of parties	What kind of Conveyance	Consideration
Joseph Hoke of Madison Co., Miss territory by his attorney to Joseph Lever	deed by letter of attorney	90
John & Catharine Drehr to Joseph Lever N C	Deed of Gift of Interest	-------
Joseph Lever B. County N C to Thomas Shuler pl.	Deed	3200
Daniel Griffin (Cooper) to John Griffin	do	250
The Same to the same	do	100
John C. Bell to Aromanus & Wm Lyles	do	800
John H. Eiffert to John P. Bond	do	150
Aaron Arms O D to John P. Bond	Lease & Release	Ł 10
Leonard Bough to Henry Miller	Deed	$200
John Bynum (Columbia) to Henry Miller	do	85.50
James Cayce to Gabriel Friday	do	500
Amos Banks Esqr to James Cayce	Sheriff Titles	180
Gabriel Fridig to James Cayce	deed	500
George Weaver Plr. to Henry Weaver do	Lease & Release	S5
Michael Oswalt to Henry Weaver	do	10
Henry Oswalt to Henry Weaver	Deed	Ł 10
Henry Oswalt to Henry Weaver	do	8
Robert Spence to Henry Weaver Junr	do	$200
George Rall & John Gertman to Henry Weaver	do	100
William Jones from heirs only to Frederick Gelzeel(?)	do	10
John Quattlebom to Lewis Hartley	do	200
Stephen Cumbo to Wilkes B. Watters	do	1000

121

Quantity & where	When Executed	What time Proved & Acknowledged
93 acres between Saluda & B. River	28th Sept 1816	26th June 1819
in a Tract of Land on Saluda	3rd May 1819	26 June 1819
93 acres in 3 Several Tracts Saluda River	7th May 1819	26 June 1819
1200 acres Publick Road to Charleston	24th Augt 1819	7th Septr 1819
500 acres on Black Creek	do	do
Lot in West Granby Congaree River	11th Decr 1818	7th Septr 1819
657 acres on Black Creek	5th Augt 1819	14th Augt 1819
100 acres on Black Creek	7th Feby 1795	20 April 1795
3 acres of a corner of a Tract of land	12 July 1819	12th July 1819
171 acres waters of Saluda River	6th June 1818	4th January 1819
in Lexington half of 1000 acres undivided cross of the road Augusta & Spring hill	23 Octr 1819	27th Octr 1819
A tract at the forks of the road Winchels	13th Jany 1819	28th Jany 1819
half of 950 acres X Road Augusta & Spring Hill	23 Sept 1819	19th Nov 1819
272 on Holly Creek waters of Twelve Mile	4th Jany 1790	4 January 1794
100 acres Lexington Dist	17th Decr 1793	18th Decr 1793
50 acres on Clemens Creek	23rd Decr 1800	9th May 1801
63 acres Clemens Creek waters of Saluda	do	do
250 acres Twelve Mile Creek waters of Saluda	18th Sept 1809	18th Septr 1809
316 acres Twelve mile Creek Wts Saluda	23rd Feby 1811	6th March 1811
100 acres	19th Jany 1819	14th Nov 1819
30 acres	8th March 1819	1st May 1819
475 acrds waters of Big Saluda	3rd Feby 1819	1st Nov 1819

Names of Parties	What kind of Conveyance	Consideration
Philemon Watters Esqr to William Calk	Lease & release	S5
Thos T Willison C E to James Seibels	Title	------
Benjamin Loveless to William Pool	Deed	L 15
Abraham Baughman to William Pool	do	$85
Samuel Walker to John W. Lee	do	500

Quantity & where	When Executed	What time Proved & Acknowledged
100 acres S side Saluda & 2 Small Islands	18th Feby 1789	13th June 1789
4146 acres of his fathers Estate land	20 Feby 1819	14th Decr 1819
150 acres between Congaree and Bull Swamp	31st Jany 1806	16th December 1819
232 acres on little Creek waters of Congaree	11th Jany 1814	16th December 1819
250 acres Lightwood Creek	21st April 1819	2rd Nov 1819

A H Fort Returns to Secretarys office
Registered in the Office of Mesne Conveyance
ending 1st January 1823

Parties	Kind of Deed	Consideration	No of acres or other property
Frederick Lites from George Snider	Deed	$50	51 acres
Jacob Corley from Jesse See	Gift	for cattle	2 head
Nancy Wing, Polly Wing, Bersheba Wing & John Wing from Ruth Taylor	Gift	cattle & other furniture	-------
James Hendrix from Alexander Jenkins	Deed	$1,000	160 acres
Do from Do	Do	$100	57 acres
George Gable from Valentine Gable	Do	$200	100 acres
John H. Eiffert from George Haltiwanger Shff	Title	$2	200 acres
Do Do from Do Do	Do	$50	500 acres
Do Do from Do Do	Do	$1.12½	50 acres
Asel R. Able from Elisha Busby	Deed	$760	340 acres
Same from John Cattle	Do	$50	70 acres
George P.(?) Lester from Abraham Merit	Mortgage deed	$5	Horses, cattle, furniture & C & C
Jacob Boozer from Wm Boozer & wife	Deed	$500	196 acres
Jacob Corley from Commisr of Equity Columbia District	Title	$485	196 acres
Thomas Burket from Jacob Souter	Deed	$1250	175 acres
Thomas Shuler from John Shuler	Do	$500	175½ do
Thomas Shuler from Mary Nicholas	Do	$260	175 do
Thomas Shuler from John Weed & Matthias Coogler	Do	$64	42 do
Conrod Slice from Samuel Busby	Mortgage	$100	74 do
Anna Wise from Jacob Tyler	Release	$20	30 do

125

The following memorial of Deeds and other conveyances
in the District of Lexington for the year

Where lying	When Executed	Proved	Recorded
Lexington waters of Saluda	30 December 1820	16 Nov 1821	1st January 1822
Lexington District	2nd January Do	2nd January do	2nd January do
Do Do	1st January do	1st January do	1st January do
Do Saluda River	27th October 1818	12th Jany 1821	4th Jany 1822
Do Do	Do Do	Do	Do Do
Do Do	5th January 1822	5th Jany do	5th do do
Lexington Black Creek sold as the property of J. Sharp	6th October 1821	8th Oct 1821	7th January 1822
Lexington sold as the property of Thos Davis	7th May 1821	3rd Nov 1821	8th Jany do
Lexington sold as the property of John Bowling	4th October 1821	3rd Nov 1821	8th Jany do
Lexington N Eidsto	23rd Oct 1820	3rd Feby 1821	8th Jany 1822
Lexington North Edisto	18th Oct 1820	3rd Feby 1821	8th Jany 1822
Lexington	13th Dec 1821	24th Jany 1822	28th Jany 1822
Lexington waters of Saluda	3rd October 1816	8th March 1817	28th Jany 1822
Lexington real estate of Jacob Boozer	7th Jany 1822	26th Jany 1822	28th Jany 1822
Do Dutch fork	3rd Oct 1808	23rd Jany 1822	29th Jany do
Do	9th March 1821	9th March 1821	Do Do do
Do Do	23rd Jany 1822	28th Jany 1822	29 Jany 1822
Do Do	9th October 1821	23rd Jany 1822	Do Do Do
Do Do	26th Jany 1822	29th Jany 1822	Do Do Do
Do Savannah Hunt Creek	30th Sept 1819	12th Jany 1822	30th Jany 1822

Parties	Kind of Deed	Consideration	No of acres or other property
Daniel Smith from Catharine Coughman, Daniel Drafts, Jacob Drafts & Jacob Kelly	Deed	$84	78 acres
William See from Commssr in Equity Columbia District	Title	$821	100 do
John Crout from John Hallman	Deed	$130	30 do
Lee & Patrick from George Haltiwanger Esqr Shff L D	Title	$60	100 do
Henry Muller from Godfrey Kirsh	Mortgage	$9,220	220 acres
Henry Muller from James Cayce	Do	$1425.87	3 negroes Jack, Sunday, & Peter
Micajah Martin from George Haltiwanger Sheriff L D	Bill of sale	$15	1 negro fellow Sip
Micajah Martin from Same	Do	$500	Do names Steve
Jacob Rall from same	Title	$100	100 acres
John C. Sharp from Thomas Burket	Mortgage	$250	5 negroes
Mary Wingard & Sarah Wingard from Elizabeth Brown	Gift		30 acres
Jacob Rall & West Caughman from George Haltiwanger Shff	Title	$101.25	50 acres
Jacob Rall & West Coughman from same	Title	$200	200 do
Jesse Drafts from Christian Hide	Deed	$300	125 do
John Snelgrove from Benjamin Page	do	$232.56¾	100 do
James Calk & Saul Simons from Barbara Corley	Do	$150	½ acre
George Leaphart from John Wessinger	Mortgage	$100	68 acres
John & Michael Fulmer from William Fulmer	Gift	Love	100 "
William Senn from Thomas Buller	Deed	$500	105 "
Jacob Buzby from Mary A. Buzby	Gift	Stock cattle & Horses	

Where lying	When Executed	Proved	Recorded
Lexington District	15th May 1820	1st Augt 1820	9th Feby 1822
Lexington Est. of Jacob Boozer	7th Jany 1822	6th Feby 1822	6th Feby 1822
Lexington District Hollow Creek	9th August 1815	26th Augt 1815	4th March 1822
Do sold as the property of Samuel Smith	7th Jany 1822	6th March 1822	7th March 1822
Lexington Congaree Low grounds	28th Feby 1822		18th March 1822
Do Granby	14th Feby 1822		Do Do Do
Do District	4th March 1822	27th March 1822	28th Do Do
Do Do	Do Do	Do Do	Do Do
Do Do	6th August 1821	29th March 1822	30th March Do
Do Broad River	29th June 1821		3rd April 1822
Do	20th March 1822	20th March 1822	3rd April 1822
Do property of Dennis Hayes	4th Feby 1822	29th March 1822	3rd Do Do
Lexington Hollow Creek	Do Do	Do Do	Do Do
Do Do	20th March Do	20th March 1822	5th April 1822
Do	5th Jany Do	4th Feby do	11th April do
Lexington Village	20th Nov 1821	13th Apl 1822	16th April Do
Lexington	17 Apr 1820	? ?	16 April 1822
fork	22nd Dec 1821	5th Jany 1822	Do
Lexington	1st Decr 1822	23rd March 1822	17th do
Do	18th March 1822	6th April 1822	17th do

Parties	Kind of Deed	Consideration	No of acres or other property
George Riser from William Dent	Deed	$2500	1224
George Leaphart from Thomas Burket	Mortgage	1500	4 Slaves
John Dent from John Crout	Deed	225.97	45 acres
Henry Senterfit from Micajah Martin	do	77.50	100 do
Same from same	do	250	400 do
George Rall from George Price	do	75	15 do
George Crapps from George Rall	do	500	111 do
Micajah Martin from G. Haltiwanger Shff	title	50	500 do
Eli Kennerly from George Lorick	mort.	100	500 do
Same from same	do	378.80	-------
Martin Hook Jun from George Lever	deed	475	60
Same from Matthias Senn	do	500	93
George Kaigler from David Kaigler	Deed	$750	250 acres
Same from same	do	4000	60
Same from same	do	300	900
Henry Muller from John T Seibels	mortgage	1096	four negroes Granby
John Taylor from John Patton	deed	1000	1081 acres
Same from Elizabeth Bell	do	4000	82 acres
James H Taylor from A Geiger & wife	do	4420	850
David Hendrix from Yost Mettze	Lease & release	₤ 15	70 acres
Same from same	Deed	$60	35
Same from John Carnline	do	200	285
Same from Sion Perry	do	200	80

129

Where lying	When Executed	Proved	Recorded
Do	1820	10th do	17 do
Do	30th Jany 1818	23 April 1822	25th Apl 1822
Do	4th do	28th Feby 1822	8th May 1822
do	12 March 1821	21st Apl 1822	do
do	15th Apl 1822	do	do
do	31st Octr 1816	1st Nov 1817	16th do
do	17 Jan 1822	17th May 1822	Do
do	4th March 1822	20th May 1822	20th May 1822
do B River	31 Feb 1822	24th May 1822	25th May 1822
do	Do	do	do
Do Saluda	9th Nov 1816	25th Mar 1817	28th do
do	7 do 1820	14 Decr 1820	do
Lexington	21st Jany 1822	29th May 1822	31st May 1822
Congaree Do	Do	Do	Do
Do	Do	Do	Do
Granby	4th June 1822	-----	20th June 1822
do	7th Jany 1822	17th June 1822	22nd do
do 3 tracts	1st Jany 1822	22nd June 1822	22nd June 1822
Congaree	do	do	24th do
Lexington waters of Saluda	15 Dec 1801	13th Mar 1802	27th June 1822
do	4th Jany 1812	21st Jany 1815	do
do	9th do	do	28th do
do	4 May 1822	18 May 1822	do

Parties	Kind of Deed	Consideration	No of acres or other property
Thos K Poindexter from G. Haltiwanger Shff	titles	20.50	44
William Currie from Daniel S. Russell	mort.	725	75
Jacob Crout from John Crout	Release	₺ 1	100
Same from Jacob Drafts	Deed	$10	20
Same from same	do	50	200
Same from Henry Taylor	do	5	100
Same from John Taylor Gun Stocker	do	50	311
Jacob Crout from Wm Sweetenberg	deed	$100	100 acres
George Leaphart from Elizabeth Geiger	do	160	one 1/3 tract of 200 acres
Adam Wacter from Zachariah Unger	do	300	100
James Clitherall from Philip Henry	Lease & Release	₺ 3400	2400
William Taylor from John Ramsay & David Campbell assigness of Clitherall & wife	release of conveyance	773	2400
Samuel Buzby from G. Haltiwanger Shff	titles	$5	426
John Meetze from Samuel Buzby	deed	22	do
Micajah Martin from Robert Allen, John Pepper of Pendleton	Do	200	2 1/6 prts of land the estate of Jesse Allen Lightwood Creek
same from Charely Davis	do	200	her part being the widow
Sarah Howard from her husband	Gift	------	125
George Lindler from Thos Boyd Esqr	Deed	416	98 acres
George M Fulmer from G Haltiwanger Shff	title	10	100
Elizabeth Bell from John Patton	Deed	625	525
Henry Neese from Charles Spears	do		25

Where lying	When Executed	Proved	Recorded
-----	24th Oct 1820(?)	27th June 1821	do
B River	9th Jany 1822	27th do	2nd July do
Lexington	31st May 1797	25th July 1801	5th do
Do	20 Feby 1814	25 Jany 1815	do
do	20 do	11 do	do
do	30th Jany 1817	Aug 16th 1817	do
Black Creek	23 May 1816	28th June 1816	8th do
Lexington	15th Jany 1819	18th Jany 1819	8th July 1822
do	1st July 1822	10 July 1822	12 do
do	1st Feby 1822	14th Jany 1822	15th do
do Sandy Run Creek	20 Nov 1796	------	26th July 1822
do	6th Apl 1822	22 Apl 1822	26th do
do waters of Edisto property of Crafts	24th Octr 1821	23 July 1822	27 do
do	8th June 1822		27 do
Do Lexington	21st March 1821	21st March 1821	7th Augt 1822
Do	Do	Do	Do
do on Pond Branch	8th May 1822	8th May 1822	10th do
do dutch fork	13th Nov 1818	20 do 1820	do
do property of Wm Fulmer	5th Augt 1822	5th Augt 1822	do
Lexington District	25th feby 1821	do	do
do	7th feby 1814	28th Apl 1814	15th do

Parties	Kind of Deed	Consideration	No of acres or other property
Henry Neese from Peter Brown of Abeville	do	61	------
John Bowland from ? ? Charles Harrison	do	₤ 25	200
John Griffin from John Heusery	Deed	$200	200
Martin Witt from Luther Smith	do	600	640
William Taylor from Catharine Rall	Gift	Love to her son	Negroe Girl Esther
Matheas Oswalt from Catharine Rall	Deed	₤ 45	113
Stephen Senterfit from Mathias Oswalt	Lease & Release	₤ 30	113
Micajah Martin from Elizabeth Senterfit & children	Deed	$400	113
Sanders Glover order to Macajah Martin(?) Comr in Equity Colia. Dist.	titles	86	1000
Mich. Martin from Elizabeth Taylor & F Singly & others	Deed	480	50
Same from George Burnet & wife	do	200	100
John U Coogle from Lewis Stack	do	12.50	12½
Joseph Coogle from Maths. Coogle	do	25	25
Leaphart & Hook from Goldthwaite & Mrs. B. Corley	do	150	½
Wm. J. Hicks from Henry Roof	do	200	25
John Lewallen from James Cronan	do	₤ 10	180
Geo L. Smith from Lewallen	do	Dower	180
Brinkley Dickerson from Smith	do	$150	180
Daniel Drafts from Ruffs	Sale	$1200 for Negroes	4 negroes
John Meetze from Barbara Corley	Deed	150	½ acre
John Meetze from Barbara Corley	do	do	do
Wm Snelgrove from Abner Snelgrove	Gift	Love	goods & chattels

133

Where lying	When Executed	Proved	Recorded
narrow of B swamp	1st Decr 1821	15 Augt 1822	do
Orangeburgh Rocky Creek	1st Apl 1796	1st Apl 1796	21st Augt 1822
Lexington bull swamp	7th Oct 1817	22nd Augt 1822	24th Augt 1822
do	29 Mar 1822	5th July 1822	5 Septr 1822
Lexington	16th Augt 1822	2nd Sept 1822	5th do
do	30 Decr 1797	30 Decr 1797	do
do	24 Feby 1800	15 Septr 1801	do
do	12 March 1821	31 Augt 1822	7th do
Lexington to effect Div. Lestergettes Estate	19 July 1819	31 Augt 1822	11th do
Lexington	27th May 1820	do	do
do	21 March 1821	8th May 1821	do
Dutch fork	6th feby 1822	25 Septr 1822	28 do
do	25 Septr 1822	26 do	Do
Village at Court H.	30 do	1st Octr 1822	1st Octr do
18 mile Creek	13 Septr 1822	4 do	4th do
18 mile Creek	13 Septr 1822	4 do	4th do
Congaree Creek	4 Nov 1796	12 Feb 1796	11 Nov do
do	8 Decr 1804	-------	do
do	Septr 1818	19th Septr 1818	do
Lexington	18 Decr 1821	15 Octr 1822	15 Octr 1822
Village	23 May 1820	23 May 1820	17th do
Do	9th Octr 1822	9th Octr 1822	18th do
Lexington	11th May 1822	7th Octr 1822	do

134

Parties	Kind of Deed	Consideration	No of acres or other property
Abner Snelgrove from Wm Snelgrove	Do	Do	Do
Daniel S. Russell from Wm Currie	deed	1500	25 acres
Jesse Fox from Stephen Johnson	Do	150	400
John Mathis from F. Sweetenberg	Do	84	9½
Elizabeth Passinger from Jacob Rall Jr	do	200	100
her children from Elizabeth Passinger	Gift	Love	100
John Livingston from Solomon Martin	Deed	$150	336
Henry Kyzer from David Weaver	Do	100	50
Richard Caver from Henry Caver	do	130	153
Katharine Keisler from Heirs of Keisler	do	----	130
A. H. Fort from George Wingard	do	500	110
Jno H High from Heirs of Younginger	Do	120	119
Willis Hughes from Joel Williams	do	100	360
John Meetze from B Corley	Do	150	½
Jacob Drafts from G. Haltiwanger Shff	Titles	$51	25 acres of H. Ruff
Davis Austin from A Banks Shff	do	52	37 acres
Davis Austin from Michael Hamiter	deed	1500	150
Davis Austin from Alexr Vick	do	40	45
Davis Austin from Swygerts admrs.	do	92	25
Daniel Rambo from Drury Sawyer	do	1000	300
Rudolph & Daniel from James Cayce	do	1200	500
James Dunbar from John Griffin	do	100	964
Same from Same	do	130	200

135

Where lying	When Executed	Proved	Recorded
Do	Do	Do	Do
Do B River	19 Jan 1822	15 Feby 1822	do
Do Lightwood Creek	14th March 1822	2 Apl 1822	do
Do B River	26 Apl 1820	26 Apl 1820	do
Do Saluda	17th May 1821	3 Octr 1821	30 do
Do	15 Jany 1822	20 March 1822	do
Do waters of Edisto	23 Octr 1821	24 Octr 1821	dl do
Do Holly Creek	16th Do 1822	9 Octr 1822	9th Nov 1822
Do Beaver Creek	20 Nov 1821	12 do	14 do
Lexington waters of Saluda	1st Apl 1814	1st Apl 1813	19 do
Do 14 mile Creek	7 Decr 1821	29 July 1822	do
Fork	1st Feby 1822	23 March 1822	20 do
Lexington waters Edisto	20 July 1821	22 July 1821	3 December 1822
Village	16th Nov 1822	6th Decr 1822	13th do
Lexington	7 Decr 1822	16 Decr 1822	16 Decr 1822
Lexington & Edgefield	6 Jany 1820	23 Decr 1822	24 Decr 1822
Lexington Hollow Creek	21 Nov 1820	23rd Decr 1822	Do
Do H Creek on Charlestown Road	24th Octr 1820	Do	Do
Do	-----	1821	Do
Do Lick Creek	24 Decr 1816	24th Decr 1816	26 do
Do Augusta Road near C ferry	13th Apl 1822	15th Apl 1822	30 do
Lexington B Creek	22 Augt 1822	28th Apetr 1822	do
Scouters Creek	26 Augt 1822	21st Septr 1822	do

Parties	Kind of Deed	Consideration	No of acres or other property
James Calk from Saul Simons	do	150	½ of ½ acres Lot

Where lying	When Executed	Proved	Recorded
Village	15 Aug 1822	20th Augt 1822	31 do

A Memorial of deeds Recorded in

From whom purchased	Purchasers Names	No. of acres	Considn.
Charles Bell	to Jacob Fulmore	75	$140.00
Thomas Boyd	David Richardson	21	30.00
Jacob Fulmore	John Gable	300	650
Comr. in Equity C. D.	Alexander Stewart	200	6750..
Jacob Stingley	John Matthias	75	150
Jacob Bright	David Briht (sic)	109	300
David Bright	Jacob Bright	for 270 quit claim	
Comr. in Equity N D	Jacob Bright	100	330
George Lightner	John Swygert	66 2/3	50
John Weed	John Swygert Jun.	29	116
Michael Wessinger	Susannah Tarer	600	330
George Holtawanger Sheriff	George Harmon	130	90
Susannah Brumby	Elisha Hammond	500	1000
Federick Shaffer	Christopher Wiggers	55	169.50
Andrew Geiger	George Leaphart	192	425
Henry Senn	George Leaphart	37	37
George Holtawanger Sheriff	Sion Waters	560	51
Godlep Sox	Mary Sharp	249	300
Sheriff of Lexington	John W. Lee	102	265
Adam Betinbaugh Snr.	Thomas Boyd	52	100
Magdalena Shroder	William Summer	42	120
Sheriff Lexington	Jacob Countz	900	50.50
Daniel S. Russell	Jacob Buzby	75	1000
Sheriff of Lexington	Jacob Countz	42	60
Samuel Kenerly	Samuel Hufman	162½	3000
Samuel Morris	Samuel Kenerly	1600½	1200
William Geiger) Jesse Geger &) Emanuel Geiger)	Samuel Kenerly	112	2254
George Hoot	Samuel Kenerly	269	1100
Barbara Corley	Daniel McGill	1/8	37.50
Barbara Corley	Rain Jenkins	½	75
John Halman	John S. Addy	25	200
Samuel Oswalt	Jacob Leaphart	180	200

Lexington District for the year 1824

Where laying	When Executed	When proved & ack.
On waters Saluda	Augt. 12 1805	January 6th 1824
Broad River	Sept 28th 1816	Jany 6th 1824
Saluda River	Decm 6th 1823	Do 6th 1824
Broad River	Sept 16th	Do. 7th 1824
in fork of B & S Riv.	January 2nd 1824	Do. 12th Do.
Do Do B & S River	April 27th 1819	Jany. 15th Do.
Broad River	Do 20th Do	Do 17th Do.
Crims Creek Dutch Fork	May 6th 1820	Do 21st Do.
Broad & Saluda R.	Do 20th 1809	January 21st 1824
Broad River	December 5th 1821	Do 21st 1824
the waters of Congaree Creek	Do 20th 1816	Do 22nd 1824
waters of Saluda	January 22nd 1824	January 23rd 1824
waters of Edisto	September 26th 1822	Do 28th Do.
Watrree branch	February 23rd 1821	Feburary 2nd 1824
waters of Saluda	May 2nd 1820	Do 3rd 1824
waters of twelve mile creek	January 10th 1816	Do 3rd 1824
waters of N Edisto	March 3rd 1823	February 24th 1824
	January 12th 1822	March 8th 1824
waters of Saluda	March 12th 1824	Do 13th Do
wat. of Broad Riv.	Do 1st 1819	Do 23rd 1824
in the fork of Brod & Saluda R	January 22nd 1822	April 16th 1824
on holly Creek	April 6th 1824	Do 17th Do
on Broad River	November 1823	Do 19th 1824
waters Do Do	April 6th 1824	April 20th 1824
Saluda River	Januay 1st 1823	Do 29th Mortgage 1824
big Do Do	October 12th 1822	Do 29th 1824
Saluda River	January 3rd 1820	April 29th 1824
the fork of Broad & Saluda River	September 30th 1817	Do 30th Do
waters of Saluda	November 20th 1823	April 30th 1824
waters of Do	September 4th 1824	Do 30th 1824
waters of Saluda	December 24th 1819	April 30th 1824
waters of Saluda	August 25th 1821	April 30th 1824

From whom purchased	Purchasers Names	No. of acres	Considn.
Jacob Leaphart	John S. Addy	180	200
John Halman	John S. Addy	41	70
Elizabeth Oswalt	Samuel Oswalt	180	20
Christian Gable	John Halman	75	262
Mary Friday	William Kinsler	687	800
Rivers Gunter	Thomas H. Spraggins	75	100
Sheriff of Lexington	William Kinsler	100	8
Jacob Rall) George Rall)	to the Elders of) St. Pauls Church)	7 3/4	5
Madalena Rekert	George Rekert	100	300
Thos & Burrel Hutcheson	George Lorick	640	480
Mary Malone) Eli Kenerly)	George Lorick	1167	18,000
Eli Kenerly	George Lorick	575	940
George Lyks	George Lorick	396	300
James Elkins	George Lorick	237	239
Samuel Lykes	George Monts	264	475
Elizebeth Surgener	Allen C. Stillman	19½	1
Ned Brooks	Hartwell Hart	133	150
Drury Fort	Hartwell Hart	8	20
Hartwell Hart	George Price	133	200
Hartwell Hart	George Price	72	200
George Price Snr	George Price Junr.	300½	200
Jacob Gall	John Geiger	200	120
Benjamin Jefcoat	Jacob Jefcoat	1000	200
John Snelgrove	Carey Snelgrove	50	100
Comr in Equity	James Cayce	581	1162
Abraham Geiger	William Geiger	240	50
William Geiger	Harmon Giger	Several parcels	--
Exr of Geo Riser decd	Samuel Fleming	400	285
George Ridlehoober	Jno W Lee	273	1300
Andrew Son	Jno W Lee	150	3750
Brinkly Dickison	Arthur Edwards	50	20
George & Catharine Roden	George Mayer	74	100

Where laying	When Executed	When proved & ack.
waters of Saluda	February 11th 1824	April 30th 1824
waters of Saluda	May 8th 1816	April 30th 1824
waters of Saluda	December 6th 1809	April 30th 1824
Do Do Do	April 22nd 1818	Do 29th Do
Congaree River	March 31st 1824	May 1st 1824
waters of N Edisto	September 5th 1816	Do 3rd Do
waters of Congaree River	May 12th 1824	May 15th 1824
on of Saluda (sic)	July 9th 1803	Do 28th Do
Lexington District	January 3rd 1814	May 29th 1824
in the fork of B S River	November 12th 1821	Do 31st Do
Broad River waters	February 21st 1822	Do Do Do
Do Do Do	Do Do Do	May 31st 1824
on Broad & Saluda Rivers	December 14th 1811	Do Do Do
in fork B & S Rivers	October 15th 1821	Do Do Do
waters of Saluda	December 29th 1823	June 19th 1824
Do Do Do	January 10th 1824	Do 22 Do
waters of Saluda	November 8th 1800	July 14th 1824
Do Do Do	January 23rd 1804	Do Do Do
waters of Saluda	Do 19th 1805	Do 14th 1824
Do Do	Do 19th 1805	July 15th 1824
Do Do	January 3rd 1818	Do 15th Do
waters of Congaree River	November 19th 1805	Augt 4th 1824
waters of N Edisto	August 11th 1823	Do 10th Do
waters of Saluda River	1824	Augt 10th Do
Do of Congaree	June 11th 1824	the estate of John Friday Do 11th 1824
Congaree Creek	March 29th 1824	Do Do Do
Do Do	July 10th 1824	the real estate of John Geiger August 4th 1824
Lexington Dist.; Edgefield Dist.	Sept 24th 1823	Do 23rd 1824
waters of Clouds Creek	January 9th 1824	Augt 23 Do
Dutch Fork	April 20th 1824	Augt 23rd 1824
Red Bank Creek	February 4th Do	Sept 8th 1824
on Camping Creek	April 12th 1824	Do Do Do

From whom purchased	Purchasers Names	No. of acres	Considn.
Sarah Poindexter	Yost Metz	50	150
A. K. J. Dunkin	Henry W. Hilliard	1980	519
Henry Oswalt	Brinkley Vick	114	200
Do Do	Do Do	32	100
Jacob Rall	Daniel Rall	27 3/4	50
Daniel Rall	John Lown Snr	45	200
John Lown Snr	John Lown Junr	90	200
Brinkley Vick	George Rall	152	600
George Rall	John Lown	152	500
Daniel Rall	John Lown	187 3/4	750
Jonathan Taylor	John H. Daily	25	100
John W. Lee	Andrew Son	1262	2140
John Horsey	Susannah Plymail	162	10
John Bolin	Adam Schmitz	100	300
James H. Maland	John C. Martin	3800	100
Micajah Martin	Michael Kinard	250	300
Do Do	Do Do	150	600
Eleanor Jumper	William L. Jumper	105	52
Elizabeth Jumper) David H. Jumper)	Do Do	210	105
John C. Sharp	Christian Mickler	54	378
John Patton	Zebulon Gantt	700	100
Abraham Fulmore	Adam Zigler	200	300
Sarah Spires	Thomas Wiles	1/3 200	20
John D. Sharp & Others	Christian Mickler	54	5
William H. Milton	John D. Sharp	118	128
George Crapps	Lawrence Grim	49	200
Miller & Pool &) John D. A. Murphy)	Samuel Archer	30	50
William Golden	Aberhart Halman	16	25
Rachel Smith	Do Do	16	25
Barbara Corley	William See	Lot	37.50
Stephen Dickerson	Thomas K. Poindexter	76	20
Exct. of George Riser	Jacob Rice	1200	916
John Crout	David Crout	62	200

143

Where laying	When Executed	When proved & ack.
waters of Saluda R.	July 10th Do	Sept 8th 1824
Bull Swamp Edisto	January 19th 1824	Sept 9th 1824
Beaver dam Creek, Sa	Do Do 1815	Do 14th Do
Do Do	March 6th 1818	Do Do Do
Do Do	November 26th 1812	Do Do Do
Do Do	January 2nd 1815	Do Do Do
Beaver dam Creek	October 4th 1817	September 14th 1824
Do Do	January 29th 1819	Do 15th Do
Do Do	August 25th 1821	Do Do Do
Do Do	January 1st 1824	Do Do Do
Turkey Creek, Congaree	Sept 10th do	Sept 23rd 1824
holly Creek, Saluda	April 20th 1824	October 18th do
Rocky Creek, Saluda	November 18th 1822	Do 19th do
Dutch fork	January 3rd 1824	Do Do Do
Cedar Creek Edisto	December 1st 1821	November 2nd 1824
Marlow Branch	March 3rd 1824	Do 5th Do
Lightwood Creek	Do Do Do	Do Do Do
Sandy Run	May 10th 1824	Do 17th Do
Do Do	Do Do Do	Do Do Do
Broad River	March 1st 1824	November 17th 1824
North Edisto	February 18th 1823	Do 18th Do
holin Sheads Creek Broad River	January 6th 1821	Do 23rd Do
Lexington District	March 11th 1824	Do 24 Do
Dutch Fork	Do 1st Do	Do 27 Do
twelve mile Creek	Novm. 24th 1824	November 27th 1824
Horse pen Creek	November 1819	December 6th 1824
boiling Spring Creek	December 6th 1824	Do Do Do
hell hole Creek	July 17th Do	Do 18th 1824
Do Do Do	Do Do Do	Do Do Do
Lexington C. H.	Sept 6th 1824	December 28th 1824
Red Bank Creek	January 4th 1820	Do Do Do
Twelve Mile Creek	February 22d 1820	Do 31st 1824
hollow Creek	Do 25th 1824	Do Do Do

Memorial of Deeds Mortgages & Other Conveyances Registered in the Office hundred and twenty five, ending with the year. Certified by A. H. Fort.

Grantors	Purchasers	Consideration	No. of acres
Jacob Neese	Henry Muller	$480	400
James Cayce	William Dickert	60	1
Thos T. Willisson	Jno S. Addy	242	200
Daniel Smith	Jac Bickley	350	668
Jac Bickley	Joh. Swicard	400	668
Alexan. Brown	Eman. Frydy	529.50	99
Shff. Holtiwanger	Henry Sebles	16.25	150
" "	" "	10.87½	100
" "	Bengamin Jefcoat	70	269
Christopher Roffman	Christian Hide	8	40
Abram Hite	" "	100	100
Jesse Drafts	Daniel Harmon	450	125
John Pearson bond	John Bates	300	150
David Bats	" "	600	346
Susan Tarer	Richard Baker	120	164
Shff. Haltiwanger	Elizabeth Oxner	18	112
John H. Franklow	Daniel Drehr	165	½ 165
Francis Davis	Adam Fulmer	150	150
Elisha & Mary Lee	John H. Franklow	275	1000
John W. Lee	John Countz	3151	150
Mary M. Tarer	Andrew Tarer	75	176
Andrew Tarer	Christener Tarer	300	176
John Taylor	George Taylor	30	33
Levi Hogabook	Elizabeth Butler	650	100
Jonathan Taylor	Adam Taylor	50	595 (?)
John Metze	Lewis Metze	100	108
Shff. Haltiwanger	Jacob Minick	650	140
Heirs of John Wolf Decd	Jacob Wolf & Joseph A. Wolf	1451	680½ acres in five tracts
Adam Zeigler	George A. Aimick	550	100
Wm. L. Rawls	" " "	100	92
James Cayce	Nicholas Hane	297.50	59½
Henry Ruff	Jacob Countz	500	57

Mesne Conveyance in Lexington in the year of Our Lord one Thousand eight Regr.

Where laying	When title made	When proved	When recorded
high hill branch	23 Octr 1824	2 Decr 1824	Jany 12th 1825
Granby	18 Octr 1824	6 Nov 1824	12 January 1825
N Edisto	5th Apr 1824	19 Jany 1825	22 Jany 1825
Boilings Springs	16 Dec 1819	29 Oct 1821	24 Jan "
Boilings Springs	27 Sept 1824	29 Oct 1824	24 Jany 1825
Rock House	4th Jany 1825	13th Jan 1824	28 Jan 1825
Readbank 6reek	22 Jany 1825	22 Jany 1825	31st Jan 1825
Congaree Creek	"	"	"
Ponn branch	24 Oct 1824	28 Jan 1824	1 February 1825
Hollow Creek	14 April 1802	25 Jan 1825	2 " "
" "	16 May 1807	19 Aug 1807	3 " "
" "	9 Nov 1824	29 Nov 1824	3 " "
Branches of N Edisto	2 Feb 1815	5 Feb 1815	7 Feb 1825
Waters of Nor edisto	30 Jan 1812	24 Oct 1812	7 Feb 1825
lick fork branch	5 feby 1825	5 Feby 1825	8th Feby 1825
horse Creek	10th " "	12 " "	14th " "
waters of Saluda	1st Jany 1825	7th Jany 1825	" " "
Chinquepin	24 Sept 1824	2nd Jany 1825	16 " "
black Creek	28 Jany 1825	3 Feby 1825	8th Mar "
Dutch fork	6 Jany "	12th Jany "	16th " "
" "	18th Augt 1804	8 Sept 1804	17 " "
" "	6th Apr 1815	6th Apr 1815	18 " "
Horse Creek	7th March 1825	17th March 1825	26 " "
Congaree River	17th Sept 1824	21 " "	31 " "
-------------	1st March 1825	1st March 1825	20th April 1825
Dutch fork high hill Creek	24 Apr 1824	19 Nov 1824	" " "
Crims Creek	10 Jan 1824	26 March 1825	21st " "
Savannahunt & Congaree	14 Mar 1825	25 " "	" " "
in the fork of Broad & Saluda R	28 Oct 1820	28 Oct 1820	" " "
Edwards branch	29 Decr 1824	29 Decr 1824	" " "
waters of Congaree River	5th Feby 1824	26th March 1825	" " "
Mill Creek Crims Creek	24th June 1822	26th March 1825	27th April 1825

Grantors	Purchasers	Consideration	No. of acres
Henry & Elizabeth Oswalt	Jeremiah Wingard	200	100
Shff. Bynum	James S. Guignard	1	7720
Henry R. Stark	Jeremiah Wingard	32.75	32 3/4
Jacob Swygert Exr.	John Mathias	202	50
Adam Epting	John Epting	50	44
Jacob Epting	" "	10 S	100
George Setzler	John Setzler	$367	122
Thos Long	Adam Countz	20 ₺	42
Martin Hook Jur.	Jacob Senn	$265	60
John B. Mayer	John A. Countz	100	9 3/4
George Swygert	Adam Countz	100	100
Oliver C. Bee Alabama	Uriah Mayer	1000	62
Christian Hankle	Jacob J. Faust	3000	262
Shff. Haltiwanger	James Kennerly	401	400
James Kennerly	Thos K Poindexter	1400	400
Jacob J. Faust Mort.	Christian Hankle	1	250
Barbara Corley	John H. Drafts	150	½
George Taylor	Daniel Lomanack	5	5
Shff. Banks	George Leaphart	195	100
" "	" "	97	100
" "	" "	210	150
" "	" "	10	100
" "	" "	5	60
" "	Wm Holeman	25	57
" "	" "	201	165
" "	Thos Wilds	31.50	460
John Shealy Senr	John Shealy Jur.	200	154
John D A Murphy	Arthur H. Fort	7.50	16
David Coogle	Daniel Metze	100	75
Shff Banks	Reuben Roof	$25	170
" "	Geo Eigleberger	100	125
" "	Geo Eigleberger	360	246
Samuel Archer	Jeremiah Harmon	550	150

147

Where laying	When title made	When proved	When recorded
Hollow Creek	28 Feb 1825	12 Apr 1825	5 May 1825
Congaree Creek	11 Dec 1801	18 June 1824	30 April 1825
------------	1 Sept 1824	7 March 1825	6 May "
Crims Creek	10 Feby 1825	5 March "	7 " "
" "	27 Augt 1821	27 Augt 1821	10 " "
" "	8 Decr 1790	5 March 1791	12 " "
Indian Creek	1 Jan 1824	1 Jan 1824	" " "
Crims Creek	26 Aug 1800	9 May 1806	" " "
Saluda River	23 Dec 1824	20 Apr 1825	14 " "
-----------	13 Jan 1813	20 Jany 1813	18 " "
fork of Broad & Saluda	16 June 1809	16 June 1809	" " "
Crims Creek	4 Feby 1822	30 Mar 1822	24 " "
Broad River	1 Mar 1824	2 Mar 1824	25 " "
Augusta Road	28 Jan 1824	29 Jan 1824	1 June 1825
" "	11 Dec "	5 Mar 1825	" " "
Broad River	1 Mar 1825	25 Apr 1825	25 May "
Lexington vill	4 June 1825	6 June "	8 June "
horse Creek	12 Mar 1825	2 June 1825	8 June 1825
waters of Twelve mile Ck.	9 June 1825	13 " "	13 " "
" " "	" " "	" " "	14 " "
" " "	" " "	" " "	16 " "
Saluda River	25 May 1825	" " "	" " "
Lexington	" " "	10 " "	28 " "
Saluda	19 Apr 1825	27 June "	29 " "
"	" " "	28 " "	" " "
waters of Cedar Creek	" " "	29 " "	30 " "
wateree Branch	15 March 1824	8 Nov 1824	" " "
fourteen Branch	22 Decr "	29 June 1825	" " "
fork of Broad & Saluda	17 Apr 1824	24 Apr 1824	26 July "
Eighteen mile branch	9 June 1825	26 July 1825	" " "
In Broad River	4 July "	4 July "	27 " "
on Broad River	" " "	" " "	" " "
Sixteen mile branch	18 Nov 1824	18 Nov 1824	28 " "

David Hendrix	Henry Hendrix	50	30
Evans Permenter	Jacob & Jesse Comalander	200	306
Sheriff Culpepper	Rignal Williams	₤ 35 0 0	150
John Sheally Senr	David Sheally	300	119
Rignal Williams	Godfrey Harman	600	197
Shff. Banks	Fredk Harmon	76	50
" "	" "	1401	250
" "	" "	48	47
" "	" "	371	100
John Stack	John Metz	80	50
David Weaver	Abrm. King	500	400
Jacob Drafts	Hilliard Drafts	love	-------
Edwd Grigg	Jacob Lindler	200	45
William Taylor	Saml Friday	125	150
John Crout Senr	Saml Crout	175	63
Jesse Metz	Lewis Metz	170	8
Philip Hook	John C. Sharp	300	120
Christian Mickler	Christopher Sharp	378	24½
Heirs of A. Geiger	John C. Sharp	241	25 several tracts
John C. Sharp	Ann Geiger a free coloured woman	27	27
Reuben Slappy	Jac C Slappy	800	45
Geo Slappy	"	50	85 3/4
Mary Wilson	J. W. Stephens	30	62
Rachel Slice	to her children	Love	50
David Kaigler	Godfrey Kirsh	1005	100
"	"	323	19
"	"	2317	120
Hon. Jno Rutledge	John Gartman	20	200
James Hayes	Fredk Cease	475	200
James S. Guignard for Rutledge	John Shumpert	36.75	350
James Hayes	Same	50	50
John S. (stricken) E. Daniel	Martin Hook	1100	475
Geo Metz	Chaney Ellisor	600	100

twenty mile branch	13 Sept 1822	22 Decr 1823	25 July 1825
waters 12 mile Creek	11 Apr 1825	12 Apr 1824	28 July 1825
waters of Saluda	16 Mar 1789	------	29 " "
Waters of N Edisto	6 July 1825	18 Apr 1825	3rd Augt "
Beaver Dam Creek	29 Dec 1808	29 Dec 1808	5th " "
" "	9 June 1825	27 June 1825	5th " "
" "	" "	" "	" " "
" "	" "	" "	9th Augt "
" "	" "	" "	" " "
N Side Saluda	23 Jan 1817	13 Mar 1817	" " "
Pond Branch	18 Dec 1818	2nd " 1819	10 " "
Twelve Mile Creek	11 Augt 1825	11 Augt 1825	11th Aug "
Dutch fork wateree Creek	2nd Oct 1824	23 Dec 1824	12 " "
waters Blk Creek	28 Augt 1823	17 Feb "	15 " "
waters Hollow Ck.	24 Feb 1824	19 Nov "	18 " "
Saluda	21 Feb "	19 Nov "	6 Sept "
waters of B River	24 Apl 1816	24 Apl 1817	12 " "
"	27 Jan 1824	13 Mar 1824	13 " "
"	26 Augt 1824	27 Augt 1824	13 " "
weavers branch Saluda	27 July 1824	22 July 1824	13 " "
Congaree River	1st June 1824	9 Feb 1825	20 " "
Lexington	15 July 1823	16 Sept 1825	" " "
Six mile Creek	19 Sept 1825	19 Sept "	21 " "
--------------	23 " "	6 Oct "	6 Oct "
Congaree River	4 Oct 1821	9thSept "	10 " "
" "	" "	" "	" " "
" "	" "	" "	" " "
Big Hollow Creek	2nd Dec 1791	6 Dec 1792	" " "
" "	11 Feb 1824	4 Oct 1825	" " "
little " "	16 Sept 1824	24 Mar 1824	11 " "
" "	21 Feb 1824	4 Oct "	11 " "
Augusta Road	15 Dec 1823	5 Apl 1824	17 Oct 1824
Hollingsheads Ck.	20 Dec 1824	9 " 1825	24 " "

Grantors	Purchasers	Consideration	No. of acres
Shff. Banks	Wm Drennan	50	50
Several Slappy	Harmon Geiger	2000	two tracts
Michael Taylor	John Fikes	100	50
Elisha Hammond mort.	John Fox	6000	500
Samuel Buzby	Elias Slice	500	25
John Carter	Benja. Hughes	30 L	150
Shff Banks	John Berry	70	70
Preston Gilder	Susanna Leaphart	109	272
Frederick Kelly	Samuel Bookman	272	296
Jacob Cumalander	Jesse Drehr	900	50
Fred Harmon	Daniel Harmon	375	73
Barbara Corley	Alexr Stewart	150	½
Jacob Countz	Wm Sweatenburg Junr	30	¼
Wm Holeson	Zebulon Gauntt	150	100
Adam Rish	Israel Gauntt	400	500
Ned Brooks	Benjamin Hews	5 S	180
Shadrack Vansant	Joseph Lybrand	100	500
Jonathon Taylor	Joseph Lybrand	65	346
Sheriff Banks	John Meetze	275	¼
Wm Calames Junr	Henry Metze	483.87	483 8/100
John Dunkin	Wm John & Stephen Dunkin	150	308
George Bowers	Jacob Vansant	222.75	297
J. M. Howel mort.	Wade Hampton Jur.	40,000	------
Stephen Williams	Isaac Lonsdale	550	290
John Rish	John J. Able	51	50
John Gable	Thos Derick	850	300
Jacob Hallman	John Oswalt	Love	100
John Roof	Benja. Roof	600	234
John Epting Senr	John Miller	100	55
John Rall	Wm Taylor	500	100

Where laying	When title made	When proved	When recorded
Black Creek	8 Sept 1824	24 Oct 1824	25 Oct 1825
Savannahunt Creek	12 June 1824	9 July 1825	" Oct "
waters of Saluda	31 Dec 1820	14 Jan 1822	26 " "
Lightwood Creek waters of N Edisto	8 Nov 1824	8 Nov 1825	14 Nov 1825
Cedar Creek	19 Augt 1825	22 Augt 1822	" " "
lick Creek	1 Nov 1789	------	15 " "
Congaree Creek	27 June 1825	7 Nov 1825	18 " "
hollow Creek	8 May 1824	8 May 1824	19 " "
holensheds Creek	4 Apr 1825	4 Apr 1825	30 " "
uper part of Dutch fork	7 Sept "	7 Sept "	" " "
Beaver Dam Creek	23 " "	8 Nov "	" " "
Lexington vill	4 June "	30 " "	1st Dec "
Crims Creek	12 Apr 1824	14 Apr 1824	" " "
North Edisto River	30 May 1822	30 May 1822	" " "
" " "	18 Mar 1825	10 Sept 1824	2nd " "
lick Creek	7 Decr 1793	15 Dec 1793	3rd " "
Congaree Creek	23 " 1823	8 Nov 1825	5th " "
" "	16 Dec 1824	16 Oct 1824(sic)	5th " "
Lexington vill	6 Oct 1825	30 Nov 1825	8th " "
holensheds Creek	17 " "	17 Oct "	12 " "
Chinquepin Creek	21 Augt 1808	28 Nov "	15 " "
head of bighorse Creek	" " 1825	17 Dec "	" " "
several tracts in Richland & Lexington	16 Jan 1822	12 Dec "	21 " "
hollow Creek	26 Nov 1804	27 Nov 1804	24 " "
" "	7 Sept 1816	10 May 1817	" " "
" "	14 June 1825	5 Sept 1825	26 " "
Rocky Branch	19 Dec "	24 Decr "	" " "
Twelve mile Creek	11 Nov "	11 Nov "	28 " "
waters of Broad River	30 Mar 1811	30 Mar 1811	29 " "
Beaver Dam Creek	5 Dec 1825	31 Dec 1825	31 Dec 1825

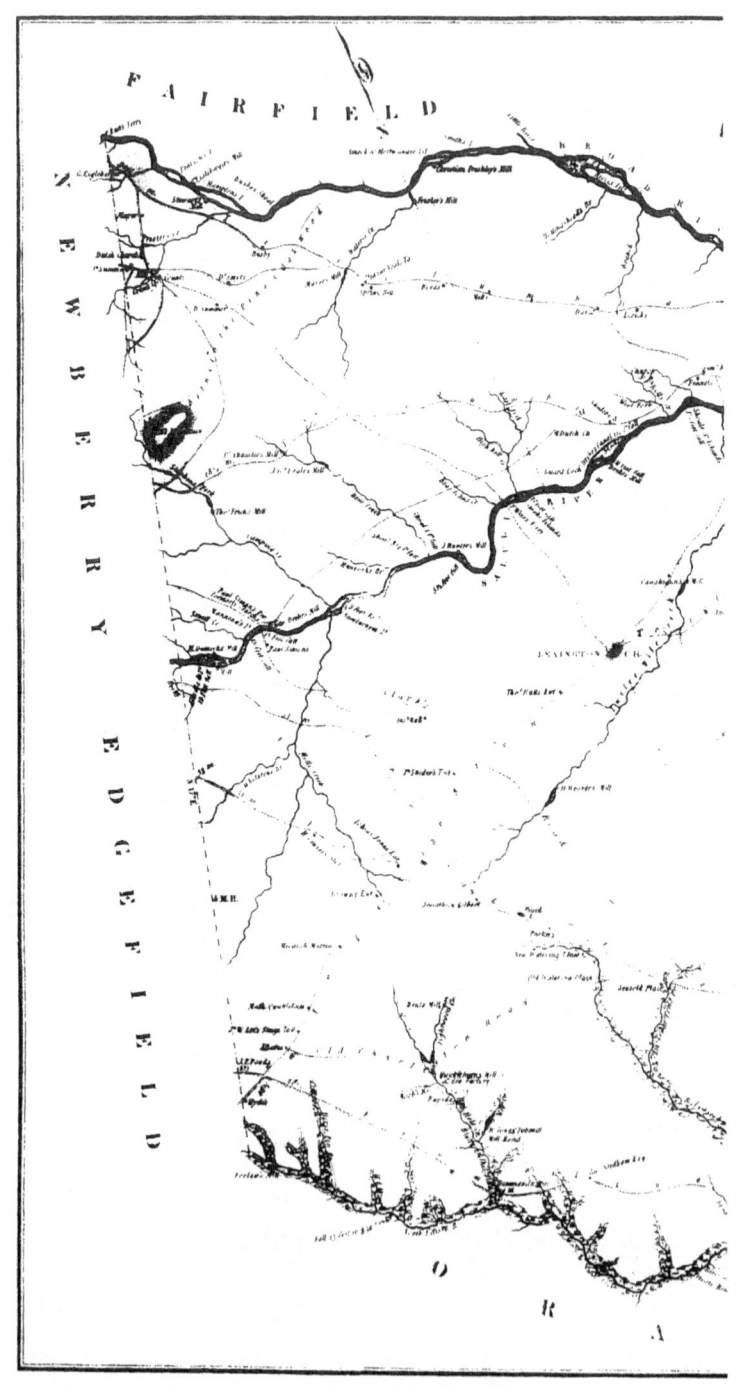

LEXINGTON DISTRICT

SOUTH CAROLINA.

SURVEYED by M. COATE, 1820

IMPROVED FOR MILLS ATLAS.

1825.

Scale 2 Miles to an Inch

GEOLOGICAL POSITION.
The upper part within the granite region covered with the primitive clay slate; the lower part lying between the lower boundary of the granite and the upper boundary of the Marine shell Limestone region.

LEXINGTON
Bearing from Columbia S 87° W 12½ Miles
Latitude North 33° 56′ 40″
Longitude West 0 15 30

Abbeville District 115
Able, Asel R 124
Able, John A 32
Able, John J. 150
Adams, Anthony 18(3)
Addy, G. 88
Addy, George 98
Addy, John S. 14, 54, 82, 138, 140(2), 144
Aimick, George A 144(2)
Airhart, Godfrey 12
Airhart, John 12
Airhart, Joseph 32
Alabama 146
Allen, Robert 130
Allen, West 20
Allman, Ezekeal 44
Amick, Adam 20(6), 112
Amick, Adam Junr 112
Amick, Catharine 20
Amick, Gasper 20, 30
Amick, Henry 20(3)
Amick, John A. 84
Ansminger, Saml 20
Archer, Samuel 8, 142, 146, 98
Arms, Aaron 120
Arthur, Ambrose 2
Arthur, Friday 62, 114
Arthur, Hargrove 4, 22
Arthur, Henry 4
Arthur, J. R. 4
Arthur, Jesse 4
Arthur, John 5
Arthur, Mary 4
Arthur, William 14
Arthur, Wm. & wf 42
Atkins, Benjamin 108
Aull, George 2, 7, 40
Austen, Davis 14
Austin, Catharine 14
Austin, Davis 5, 40(2), 134(4)
Autrey, David 8
Averhart, John 7
Awengard, John 9

Baker, Catharine 12
Baker, Joseph 98
Baker, Richard 144
Baker, William 12, 114
Baker, William Senr 94
Bales (Bates?), John 15
Bales, Wiley Bull 68
Ballard, Robert 22
Bamberg, John F. 114
Banks, A. 13, 90, 92, 100
Banks, Amos 5, 7, 9(2), 11, 17(20), 48(2), 52, 68, 76(4), 78(2), 80(2), 88(2), 90, 96, 100, 102, 104, 106, 110, 114, 118, 120, 134,
Banks, Amos Esq. 50, 52(2), 112
Banks, Charles 76
Banks, Shff 146(11), 148 (4), 150(3)
Barnett, Judah 17
Barr, M. 13
Barr, Michael 6, 8, 64, 92
Barsh, Conrad 94
Bartin, Richard 60
Bartlett, Rhody 4
Bartlett, Thomas 4, 60

Bartlet, William 88, 102
Barton, Abraham 106(2)
Bates, Catharine 90(2)
Bates, John 90, 96, 144(2)
Bates, Sarah 54, 82
Batey, John 98
Bats, David 144
Baugh, John 2
Baugh, Leonard 5
Baugh, Leonard John 2
Baughman, Abraham 122
Baughman, Jacob 62
Baughman, John 7, 18, 44, 60, 72(2)
Baughman, J. Henry 72
Baughman, Ulrick 42
Baughman, William 72
Bauknight, John 44(3), 54
Beadenbaugh, Michl 24
Beard, Anna Maria Sivley 108
Beard, Frederick 110
Beard, James 74
Beard, James & wife 48
Beasley, Shaderick 26
Beatenback, Ulrick 90
Beatenbough, Michael 74
Bee, Oliver C. 146
Beesley, Shaderick 40
Bell, Burrel 92
Bell, Charles 32, 40, 88, 138,
Bell, Elizabeth 128, 130
Bell, Jacob 14
Bell, John 92, 116
Bell, John C. 7, 82, 118(2), 120
Bellinger, Elizabeth 60
Beninger, Michl 88
Benton, John 48(2), 76(2)
Berringer, Catharine 88
Berry, Elizabeth 10
Berry, John 150
Betinbaugh, Adam Snr. 138
Bick, Jacob 7
Bickley 90
Bickley, Jac 144(2)
Bickley, Jacob 60, 70(2)
Bickley, John 6
Bickley, Nancy 6
Bickley, Uriah 7
Bickly, Jacob 9, 116
Black, Adam 12, 116(2)
Black, John 12, 15, 38(2), 44(2), 54, 72(2), 82, 116
Blackley (heirs) 72
Blake 96
Blake, John Hiag 94
Blakely, Dyonisuis 118
Blakely, Sally 44
Blocker, Abner 18, 96
Bloodworth, Samuel 108
Bloodworth, William 104
Boatwright, Daniel 64(2), 106
Boatwright, James 22, 50, 62(2), 76, 114
Boatwright, William 36
Bod, Thos 34
Boland, Abraham 32
Boldlin, Drewry 26
Bolin, John 142
Bond, John Meetze 100
Bond, John P 14, 28, 40, 68, 90, 92, 106, 120(2)
Bone, George 110

Bookman, Saml 110(4), 150
Boozer, David 4, 11, 16, 62, 78, 114(2)
Boozer, Eliza 12
Boozer, Elizabeth 78
Boozer, Elizabeth Senr 114
Boozer, Henry 62, 114
Boozer, Jacob 2, 4, 16, 64, 114, 124, 125, 127
Boozer, Wm 124
Boozer, Wm Senr 114
Bough, Fred 56
Bough, Frederick 14
Bough, Leonard 120
Boughman, Eve 118
Boughman, H. J. 44
Boughman, Harmon 118
Boughman, John 114
Boughman, John H. 60
Boughman, Wm. 44
Bouknight, Daniel 10
Bouknight, George 36(2)
Bouknight, John 7, 34(3), 36(2), 72
Bouknight, John Jr. 7, 11, 20
Bouknight, John Senr 72
Bouknight, Michael 62, 82
Bowen, Gasway 66
Bowers, George 150
Bowers, Jacob 28, 114
Bowland, Drury 100
Bowland, John 132
Bowling, John 125
Boyd, James 40, 118
Boyd, Thomas 28, 34, 138(2)
Boyd, Thos Esqr 130
Boyd, Thos Junr 94
Boyles, Thomas 26
Braselman, Drucilla 62, 76
Brasill, William 64(2)
Brasilman, Drusiller 48, 94
Brice, John 10
Brickell, James 88, 108
Bright, David 38
Bright, Jacob 38, 138(5)
Brooks, Edwards 88
Brooks, James 38
Brooks, Ned 140, 150
Brooks, Whitfield 110
Broon, Elizabeth 38
Brown, Alexan 144
Brown, Elizabeth 126
Brown, James 8
Brown, Peter 132
Brumby, Susannah 138
Brumby, R. H. 110
Bugh, Catharine 8
Buller, Thomas 126
Bundrick, Charles 48, 74
Burgess, Joseph 68, 20
Burges, Joshua 68
Burgess, William 96
Burket, Margaret 4
Burket, Thomas 4, 8, 9, 64(2), 90, 124, 126, 128
Burnet, George 132
Busbee, Jeremiah 32
Busby, Benjamin 48, 74
Busby, Elisha 124
Busby, Jacob 64(2)
Busby, Samuel 124
Busby, Shearwood 34

Bush, John 68
Butler, Elizabeth 6, 144
Butler, William 6
Buzbee, Benjamin 22
Buzby, Jacob 126, 138
Buzby, Mary A 126
Buzby, Samuel 8, 130(2), 150
Bynum, John 120
Bynum, Shff 146

Calames, Wm. Junr 150
Calk, James 15, 17, 126, 136
Calk, William 92, 122
Callaham, David 7, 18, 68, 106(3)
Callaham, James 6
Campbell, David 130
Campbell, John 110
Canty, Zachariah 68(4)
Carline, George 100
Carline, Lewis 26, 100
Carnlin, George 100
Carnline, John 40, 128
Carnline, Lewis 26(3), 32, 40
Caroline, Cristian 26
Carpenter, Jno Countz 90, 102
Carter, John 150
Cates, John 7
Cattle, John 124
Caughman, George 18, 24
Caughman, John 5
Caughman, West 4, 5(2), 24, 126
Caver, Barbara 88
Caver, Henry 88, 134
Caver, Richard 134
Caver, Samuel 66
Cayce, James 4, 7, 100(2), 114, 120(3), 126, 134, 140, 144(2)
Cease, Fredk 148
Cetsinger, Benjn 38
Chaney, Levi 32, 36
Chapman, John 100(2)
Chapman, William 100
Chapp, Jacob 14
Chargill, Thomas 114(2)
Cheesbrough, Luke Dr. 8
Chessbrough, Jonal 8
Chumperd, Peter 114
Chupp, Dennis 94
Chupp, Jacob 94
Church Wardens 60
Clark, Cornelous 34, 62
Clark, Gregory 116
Clark, Parker
Class, Frederick 56(2), 84(2)
Clements, Gabl 44, 72
Clifton, C. 92
Clifton, Claiborne 114
Clitherall 130
Clitherall, James 130
Coffill, Benjamin 108
Comalander, Jacob 148
Comalander, Jesse 148
Conheim, Charles F. 6, 68
Conheim, M. 94
Conheim, Martha 6
Coogle, David 8, 146
Coogle, John 9, 96
Coogle, John U. 132
Coogle, Joseph 132
Coogle, Maths 132

Coogle, Peter 8
Coogler, George 4
Coogler, John 4
Coogler, John Uriah 82, 54
Coogler, Mathias 4, 124
Coogler, Ulrick 28
Cook, Nathan 94, 98
Coon, Frances 20, 68
Corben, Samuel 68
Corben, Wm P 14
Corbin, Samuel 6, 14
Coryell, Jesse 36
Corley, B. 134
Corley, Mrs. B. 132
Corley, Barbara 88, 100, 104, 108,
      126, 132(2), 138(2),
      142, 146, 150
Corley, Eman1 5, 13, 96(2), 60
Corley, Jacob 62, 124(2)
Corley, Lawrence & wife 26
Corley, Manuel 17
Corley, Nathaniel 110
Corly, Barbara 13
Coughman, Andrew 90
Coughman, Catharine 126
Coughman, Christopher 96, 100
Coughman, John 90, 12
Coughman Wes 8
Coughman, West 10, 13(2), 17(2), 94, 96(3)
      126
Countz, John 2, 7
Countz, Adam 14, 146(2)
Countz, Jacob 15, 112(3), 138(2), 144, 150
Countz, John 5, 8, 66(2), 90, 102, 118,
      144
Countz, John (Carpenter) 6
Countz, John A. 146
Coursey, Lewis 24(2)
Coward, Dunsey 64
Crafts 131
Crapps, George 10, 128, 142
Crapps, John 11
Craps, John 5, 18, 22
Craps, Michael 5
Creps, George 20, 34
Crims, John 36
Crim, Laurence 36, 66(2)
Cronan, James 132
Crotwell, George 38(2), 82
Crout, David 142
Crout, Elizabeth 46
Crout, Jacob 130(2)
Crout, John 126, 128, 130, 142
Crout, John Senr 148
Crout, Saml 148
Croutwell, George 54
Crumpton, Henry T. 56, 84
Cryder, Joseph 7
Culpepper, Sheriff 148
Cumalander, Jacob 150
Cumbo, Stephen 120
Cunkle, Henry 100
Currie, William 130, 134

Dailey, James 64
Daily, James 5, 28
Daily, John H. 142
Daniel 134
Daniel, E. 148
Daniel, Elisha 2, 5, 22, 104, 114

Daniel, John S. 148
Daniel, Stephen 14
Daniel, William 15, 22(2), 54, 82
Davis, Charely 130
Davis, Drury 15, 110
Davis, Frances 90, 106
Davis, Francis 144
Davis, Needham 26(2), 28, 38(3), 58, 62, 86
Davis, Thos 125
Dayley, James 78, 50
Debardeladen, A. 36
Deckert, John 38(2)
Deckert, Michael 36
Dellet, James 22, 28, 54(2), 60(2), 76, 82(2)
      118(2)
Dellet, James Esqr 48, 114, 118
Deloach, Thos 92
Delozeair, Asa 22
Dent, John 68, 128
Dent, William 48, 76, 92, 106, 112, 116, 128
Derick, Andrew 8, 11, 15, 116(2)
Derick, Davis 100
Derick, George 8, 22, 28
Derick, Jacob 6
Derick, John 7, 9, 116(3), 118
Derick, John H. 8
Derick, Thomas 6, 116, 150
Derit, Wm 13
Derrick, Andrew 116
Derrick, George 116
Derrick, John 116
Derrick, Thomas 114, 116

Dewees, Andrew 22
Dickerson 132
Dickerson, Stephen 142
Dickert, J. 38
Dickert, John 64
Dickert, M. 38
Dickert, Michael 64
Dickert, William 144
Dickison, Brinkly 140
Dishazo, Lewis 112
Domonick, Henry 52, 78
Dougharty, James 64
Dozer, Henry 66
Drafts, Daniel 4, 28(2), 56, 84, 126, 132
Drafts, Hilliard 148
Drafts, Jacob 4(2), 26, 42, 56, 100, 108,
      130, 126, 134, 148
Drafts, Jacob Senr 84
Drafts, Jesse 126, 144
Drafts, John H. 146
Drafts, Samuel 4, 26
Drehr, Catharine 120
Drehr, Daniel 144
Drehr, Jesse 150
Drehr, John 6, 20(2), 28(2), 40, 46, 58, 74,
      86(2), 90, 114, 120,
Drennan, Wm. 150
Dublin a free black man 4
Duke, John 46, 74, 54, 82
Dunbar, James 134
Dunkin, A. K. J. 142
Dunkin, John 150
Dunkin, William 150(2)
Dunkin, Stephin 150

Earhart, Godfrey 112(3)
Earhart, John 112

Eddins, James 18
Eddins, John 106
Eddins, William 18
Eddins, Zilpha 18
Edins, Martha 84
Edins, Wm. 84
Edwards, Arthur 140
Edwards, Jeremiah 64, 106, 116
Effler, Catharine 6
Effler, Peter 6
Eiffert, John H. 1, 12, 13, 18, 112, 130, 124
Eiffert, Mary 12
Eigleberger, Geo. 6, 7, 46, 74, 104, 146(2)
Eigleberger, Katharine 104
Eitson, Elizabeth 44
Eitson, James 44
Eleazer, Henry 6, 8
Eleazer, Simeon 6, 74(2)
Eleazer, Simon 48
Elesor, Jacob 34
Elison, Jane 6
Elkins, James 140
Elleazer, Simeon 38
Ellesor, Frederick 50
Ellesor, Gasper 30
Ellisor, Chaney 148
Ellison, Frederick 78
Emick, Adam 56
Emick, Christian 56
Enlow, John 48, 74
Epting, Adam 146
Epting, David 92
Epting, George 10
Epting, Jacob 10, 146
Epting, Jacob Senr 40
Epting, John 146(2)
Epting, John Capt. 8
Epting, John Senr 150
Epting, John Adam 20
Eragle, Michael 6, 7, 60, 100(2)
Ergle, George Michl 20
Erigle, Jacob 68
Erigle, Michael 48
Ervan, James D. 76
Erwin, James 48
Evins, Henry 88(2)

Fanning, John 92
Faust, Jacob J 146(2)
Ferrick, John 28
Fetner, George 110
Fikes, George 116(4)
Fikes, John 13, 150
Fikes, Martin 13, 116
Fleming, Saml 58, 86, 106(2), 140
Folmer, Mathias 42
Fort, A. H. 10, 13, 14, 17, 96, 134,
Fort, A. H. Capt. 50
Fort, Arthur 28
Fort, Arthur H. 8, 78, 146
Fort, Drury 140
Fouts, Martin 68
Fox, Jesse 18(3), 40, 50, 76, 96, 134
Fox, John 150
Fox, Thomas Junr 50, 76, 96
Frazer, John 70
Franklow, John H. 144(2)
Franklow, John P. 76
Franklow, Sarah 76

Frazer, Jesse 34
Frazer, John 70
Frazier, Jasper 116
Free, Elizabeth 116
Free, Martin 12, 28, 40, 66(2), 94, 116
Freshley, Christian 22, 36
Freshley, John 22, 36, 70
Freshly, Christian 10
Frey, George 26
Frey, Philip Martin 26
Frick, Caty 26
Frick, Thomas 26 (2)
Friday, David 26
Friday, Emanuel 10, 62, 88
Friday, Gabriel 54, 62, 88, 108, 112(2), 120
Friday, John 7, 10, 22, 50, 78, 98, 141
Friday, Lewis 10
Friday, Mary 140
Friday, Saml 148
Fridig, Gabriel 64, 68, 80, 120
Frydy, Eman 144
Fullmer, Abrahm 78
Fullmer, Jacob 76
Fulmer, Abraham 11, 50,
Fulmer Adam 144
Fulmer, Anasticca 98
Fulmer, George M. 130
Fulmer, John 126
Fulmer, John William 98
Fulmer, Michael 126
Fulmer, Nicholas 38
Fulmer, William 126, 131
Fulmore, Abraham 142
Fulmore, Jacob 138(2)

Gable, Christian 100, 140
Gable, George 124
Gable, John 15, 22, 26, 138, 150
Gable, Valentine 40, 124
Gall, Jacob 140
Gallman, Henry 10
Gartman, Barbara 12
Gartman, Catharine 98, 100
Gartman, Catharine Junr 98
Gartman, David 56, 84
Gartman, John 66, 148
Gartman, Mary 56, 84(2)
Gartman, Philip 2
Gauntt, Israel 150
Gauntt, Zebulon 142, 150
Gaulman, Henry 106
Geatsinger, Benjn 38
Geiger, A. 14, 128, 148
Geiger, Abraham 32, 34, 36, 46, 54, 64, 74,
            82, 112, 114, 118(4) 140
Geiger, Abraham Senr 54, 82
Geiger, Abram 2
Geiger, Andrew 138
Geiger, Ann 84, 148
Geiger, Elizabeth 130
Geiger, Emanuel 138
Geiger, Harman 4, 46, 54, 72, 82, 84, 150
Geiger, Harmon H 90, 92(2), 118
Geiger, J. Harman 36
Geiger, Jacob 52, 72, 78, 92
Geiger, Jesse 8, 110, 138
Geiger, John 2, 4, 18, 44(3), 46, 60(3), 72(3),
            140, 141
Geiger, John Senr 38
Geiger, Mary Ann 82

Geiger, Nancy 8
Geiger, Randolph 26(2), 32, 36, 54,
    70, 82, 90, 92, 114
Geiger, Une(?) 110
Geiger, Wm 2, 4, 7, 8, 36, 44(2), 46,
    54, 72(3), 82(2), 84, 138,
    140(2)
Geiger, Wm Senr 36, 92
Geiger, Wm H. 40
Geiger, Wm J 8
Gelzeel (?), Frederick 120
George, Lewis 64, 90
George, Lutherick 64
George, Magdalena 64
Gertman, John 120
Gibson, denis 66, 70
Gibson, Dennis 36, 110
Gibson, John 20, 68
Gibson, Samuel 36
Gieger, Abraham 46
Giger, Harmon 140
Gilbert, Jonathan 14
Gilbert, Nancy 14
Gilder, Preston 150
Gill, John 110(2)
Gissendanner, David 62
Glover, Sanders 132
Golden, George 50, 78
Golden, William 142
Goldthwaite 132
Gough, Eva 56
Gregory, Dorathy
Griffin, Daniel 68(2), 120
Griffin, John 18, 68(2), 120, 132,
    134
Grigg, Edwd 148
Grim, John 5
Grim, Lawrence 142
Gross, Catherine 50
Gross, George 9, 50
Grubbs, Henry 90, 98, 102
Grubbs, Phillip 90, 102
Guignard, J. S. 46
Guignard, James S. 22, 28(2), 32, 62,
    66, 84(2), 88, 100,
    108, 110, 112, 146,
    148
Guignard, James Sanders 22
Gunter, Rivers 68, 140

Hails, Robert 34
Hall, Ainsley 26, 32
Hall, Jacob 62, 64, 108(2)
Hall, James 64
Hall, Joel 18
Hall, John 62, 64, 108(2)
Hall, John Junr 66
Hall, John Senr 80, 66, 32, 52
Hall, Susanah 100, 104
Hall, William 20, 28, 68, 108
Hallman 90, 102
Hallman, Jacob 98, 150
Hallman, John 24, 46, 74, 126
Hallman, Joseph 40
Hallman, Margaret 74
Hallman, Margrate 24
Halman, Aberhart 142
Halman, John 138, 140(2)
Haltiwanger 126
Haltiwanger, G. 100, 128, 130(3), 134

Haltiwanger, George 12, 15, 100, 124, 126(2)
Haltiwanger, H. F. 12
Haltiwanger, Shff 144(2), 146
Ham, Nicholas 76, 102
Hamiter, Michael 2, 134
Hammond, Elisha 138, 150
Hampton, Margaret 46, 74
Hampton, Richard 60
Hampton, Wade Jur. 150
Hamton, Thos 104
Hane, N. 5
Hane, Nicholas 18, 48, 50, 64(2), 76, 78,
    104, 118, 144
Haney, John 28, 30
Hankle, Christian 114, 146(2)
Hare, Henry 98
Haring, Rebecca 62
Harman, Christian 40
Harman, Godfrey 4, 36
Harman, Lawrence 36
Harmon, Daniel 144, 150
Harmon, Fred 150
Harmon Fredk 148(4)
Harmon, George 138
Harmon, Godfrey 26, 114, 148
Harmon, Jacob 13, 14
Harmon, Jeremiah 146
Harmon, John 64
Harmon, William 52, 78
Harris, Abraham 44, 72(2)
Harris, Abram 46
Harris, Ann 54
Harris, Dorethy 46
Harris, George 46
Harris, John 54, 82
Harris, John & wife 46
Harris, Martha 22, 46
Harrison, Charles 60, 132
Harrison, Deril 15
Hart, Benjamin 66(2)
Hart, Hartwell 140(4)
Hartley, Lewis 36, 120
Hartman, William 98
Hartzmetz, Mary 88
Hatcher, Jeremiah 15
Haugabook 106
Haugabook, Jacob 118
Haugabook, John 7, 12, 106
Haugabook, Levi 12
Havis, Ann 62
Hayes, Dennis 127
Hayes, James 148(2)
Hays, Dennis 56, 84
Hendrix, Absalom 16, 22, 34, 40, 94
Hendrix, David 13, 17, 34, 42, 56(2), 82, 84,
    128, 148
Hendrix, Elizabeth 34
Hendrix, Hannah 46
Hendrix, Henry 34, 46, 62(2), 96, 148
Hendrix, James 96, 124
Hendrix, John 34, 48, 64(2), 76
Hendrix, Peter 54, 82
Hendrix, Saml 34
Hendrix, Sarah 96
Hendrix, William 56, 60, 62(4), 82, 110
Heney, Free 36
Henry Philip 130
Henton, Moses 13
Hentz, Michael 54, 82
Herbert, Thomas 24

Herbert, Thos & wife 40
Herbert, Thomas S. 24
Herring, Nicholas 42
Heusery, John 132
Hews, Benjamin 150
Hicks, Wm J. 132
Hide, Christian 126, 144(2)
Hidle, Martin 4
Hidle, John 4
Hietle(?), John 72
High, John H. 100
High, Jno H. 134
Hill, Henry H. 14
Hill, Mary 44, 72
Hill, Theos. 15
Hilliard, Henry W. 142
Hillman, Charles L. 38
Hite, Abram 144
Hite, Christian 6
Hite, Michael 6
Hoffman, Jacob 84
Hogabook, Levi 144
Hogg, John 50, 78(2)
Hohaimer, Philip 6
Hoke, Christine 60
Hoke, David 44, 72
Hoke, Joseph 120
Hoek, Samuel 110
Hoke, William 60
Holddewanger, George 24(3)
Holeman, Wm **146**(2)
Holeson, Wm 150
Hollingshed, Saml 88
Hollman, Andrew 110(3)
Hollman, Harlley 108
Hollman, John 110
Hollman, Margaret 46
Holman, Aberhart 104
Holman, Andrew 48, 74
Holman, Harlley 108
Holman, Susannah 112
Holtawanger, George 138(2)
Holtiwanger, **Shff** 144(3)
Honold, Jacob 10
Hook 132
Hook, M. 13
Hook, Martin 54, 148
Hook, Martin Junr 82, 128, 146
Hook,Philip 84, 148
Hook, Philip & wife 56
Hooker, John 42(2), 50, 76
Hoover, George 88
Hoover, John 56, 84
Hoot, George 138
Horsey, John 142, 116
Hougabook, Levi 106
House, Nancy 62
House, Nicholas 62, 100
Houseal, Elizabeth 118
Houseal, Margt. 6
Houseal, William 118
Houseal, Wm. F. 5, 90, 102, 112
Hout, George 38, 138
Howard, Evin 18
Howard, John 18(2)
Howard, Sarah 130
Howel, J. M. 150
Howel, Jesse M. 82, 54
Hoyler, Barnet 16
Hoyler, Daniel 16
Hoyler, Gabriel 16

Huff, H. 134
Huffman, Daniel 96
Huffman, Emanuel 92
Huffman, John 44
Huffman, Jacob 6, 8, 38, 56, 62, 78, 86(4), 94, 114
Huffman, Samuel 42, 118
Hufman, John 32, 44
Hufman, Samuel 138
Hughes, Benja. 150
Hughes, Willis 134
Hughs, Benjmin 32
Hughs, Wm. 32
Hutcheson, Burrel 140
Hutcheson, Thos 140
Hutchison, Ainey 48
Hutchison, Arney 74
Hutchison, Arnold & wife 24
Hutchison, Susanah 112

Illinois Territory 110
Isley, John 24

Jackson, Rebecca 62
Jackson, sarah 94
Jacobs, John 34
Jefcoat, Benjamin 6, 28, 94, 140, 144
Jefcoat, Daniel 28, 30
Jefcoat, Jacob 26, 50, 76, 140
Jefcoat, Saml 36, 42
Jenkins, Alexr 96, 124
Jenkins, James H. 14
Jenkins, Rain 138
Johnson, Jacob 18
Johnson, Martin 18
Johnson, Stephen 20, 134
Johnston, Isaiah 112
Johnston, Joel 112
Johnston, Micajah 112
Jones, John 8
Jones, Lewis 26, 94, 110
Jones, Sarah 104
Jones, Tobias 66
Jones, Wm. 40(2), 120
Jumper, David 11
Jumper, David H. 142
Jumper, Eleanor 142
Jumper, Elizabeth 142
Jumper, Samuel 118
Jumper, Samuel Senr 22
Jumper, William L. 142

Kaigler, Andrew 2, 6, 28, 58, 86
Kaigler, David 36, 52(4), 80(10), 94, 92, 128, 148(3)
Kaigler, Elizabeth 52(4), 80(10)
Kaigler, George 18(6), 20, 40, 88, 128
Kaigler, James 88, 106
Kaigler, John 2, 18
Kaigler, Margaret 2, 28, 88
Kaigler, Michael 18(3), 20, 36
Kailer, Andrew 106
Kammoner, Jacob 108
Keabler, George E. 32
Kedle, John 44
Kedle, Polly 44
Kegler, Andrew 114
Keisler, 134
Keilser, Katharine 134
Keizler, Geo. 13
Keizler, Jacob 12

Keizler, Katharine 12
Keller, Michel 116
Kelly, Frederick 2, 48, 76, 92(2), 150
Kelly, George 12
Kelly, Jacob 10, 12, 116, 126
Kelly, John 32
Kelly, Mary 32
Kelly, Messrs 34
Kelly, Saml 13
Kennemore, Michael 24(2), 82
Kenerly, Eli 140(2)
Kenerly, Samuel 138(4)
Kenerly, Susanah 62
Kennerly, David & wife 26
Kennerly, Eli 128
Kennerly, Elisabeth 14
Kennerly, James 15, 26(3), 54, 80, 146(2)
Kennerly, Joseph 28
Kennerly, Mary 36(2)
Kennerly, Rachel C. 62
Kennerly, Saml 2, 14, 66(2), 96
Kennerly, Susana 22
Kershaw, Joseph 42
Kinamon, Michael 54
Kinard, Jacob 50
Kinard, Michael 96, 142
Kinard, Samuel 24
King, Abrm 148
King, Ellener 40
King Susanah 40
Kinsar, William 88
Kinsler, Anna 68
Kinsler, John 112
Kinsler, William 11, 14, 54, 62, 64, 68(3), 80, 102, 112, 140(2)
Kirsh, Godfrey 9, 126, 148(3)
Kleckley, Jacob 9(2)
Kleckley, John 8(2)
Koon, Barbara 110
Koon, Frances 68, 106
Koon, Jacob 2, 110
Koon, John Henry 2
Koon, samuel 2, 7, 8
Kreps, Daniel 60
Kreps, Michael 94, 100,110(2)
Kunkle, Henry 7, 48, 74
Kynard, Jacob 78
Kyzer, Christian 46, 74(2), 98, 108(2)
Kyzer, David 16, 98
Kyzer, Henry 108(2), 110, 134
Kyzer, John 110
Kyzer, Ulrick 38

Lampkin, Peter 66
Lance, Lambert 22
Langford, James 92
Langley, Isham 106
Lansdale, Abraham 18
Lansdale, Isaac 38
Laurens District 115
Leaphart 132
Leaphart, George 9, 98, 126, 128, 130, 138(2), 146(5)
Leaphart, Jacob 138, 140
Leaphart, John 26(3)
Leaphart, Susanna 150
Leard, Mary 26
Leaver, John 22
Leaver, Saml 22, 82
Lee 126
Lee, Elisha 144

Lee, John 48(2), 74, 76
Lee, John L. 140
Lee, John M 9
Lee, John W. 5, 15, 20, 50, 52(2), 78, 80(2), 96, 100, 104, 106(2), 122, 138, 140, 142, 144(2)
Lee, Mary 144
Lee, William H. 10, 34(2), 40
Leech, David 108
Lefloor, Ann 28
Leits, Frederick 116
Lemar, Thomas 15
Leonard, John 4
Leonard, Thomas B. 4
Lever, George 128
Lever, Joseph 120(3)
Lever, Samuel 54
Lester, G. D. 56
Lester, George D. 84, 80, 52
Lester George P(?) 124
Levingston, John 32, 56 Sr. 56, 84
Lewallen 132
Lewallen, John 132
Lewey, Henry 78
Lewy, Henry 50
Lightner, Abigail 4
Lightner, Christian 4, 50, 52, 64, 76, 80
Lightner, Daniel 15
Lightner, George 138
Lightner, John 20(2)
Liks, George 68
Lindler, George 9, 13, 15, 64(2), 130
Lindler, Jacob 28, 38, 148
Lipp, John 110
Lipps, John 106, 110
Lites, Frederick 124
Lites, Jacob 24, 32, 34, 54, 82
Lites, Joseph 48(2), 76
Litter, John 92
Livingston, Barnet 16, 84
Livingston, John 134
Livingston, William 16, 106(2)
Lloyd, J. W. 36
Lomanick D. 13
Lomanack, Daniel 98, 146
Lomonack, Jacob 116
Long, Christian 74
Long, Christian & wife 48
Long, George 32 (5), 106
Long, Thos 146
Lonsdale, Isaac 150
Loreman, John 36
Lorick, George 7, 74, 96, 128, 140(5)
Lorick, John 118 Jacob 68
Lorick, Michael 46(2), 74(5)
Lott, Mark 106
Lott, Mark Junr 106
Lott, Mark Senr 106
Louck, Michael 16
Lourick, Michl 46
Loveless, Benjamin 122
Lowerman, Ann Katharine 12
Lowerman, George 12
Lowerman, Jacob 12, 14
Lowerman, John 4, 12, 44, 72
Lowerman, William G. 4
Lown, John   142(2)
Lown, John Junr 142
Lown, John Senr 142(2)
Loyd, Joseph W. 36

Lucas, Jacob 66
Luts, Jacob 13
Lybrand, Baroned 44
Lybrand, Barnet 72, 10
Lybrand, Henry 13
Lybrand, Isaac 6, 17
Lybrand, John 7
Lybrand, Joseph 116(2), 150(2)
Lybrand, Martin 12, 96
Lybrand, Wm 7, 44, 72
Lykes, Samuel 140
Lyks, George 140
Lyles, Aromanus 120
Lyles, Susanah 48, 76, 94
Lyles, William 120

McCreless, John 6, 16, 22, 28, 30, 34, 104, 118
McCreless, John (ordinary) 2, 4
McGill, Daniel 138

Madison Co., Miss 120
Maland, James H. 142
Malone, Mary 140
Manning 92
Manning, Luke 92
Marshall, M. A. Warying 90
Martin, John C. 98, 100, 142
Martin, Micajah 5, 42, 52, 56, 80, 66, 84, 94(2), 100, 106, 116 126(2), 128, 142, 130, 132(3)
Martin, Soloman 62, 68, 134
Matheson, John 50, 78, 80
Mathias, John 6, 8, 146
Mathias, Jonas 6
Mathias, Sarah 6
Mathis, John 134
Mathison, John 52
Matthias, Jonas 66
Matthias, John 80, 138
May, Joseph 38
Mayer, Adam 15, 88
Mayer, Benedict 6(2), 24(3), 112
Mayer, Eve M. 112
Mayer, George 13, 98, 140
Mayer, J. B. 24(8)
Mayer, Jacob 13, 98(2)
Mayer, John Adam 6,
Mayer, John B. 146
Mayer, John Benedict 20
Mayer, Margt 6
Mayer, Uriah 15, 62, 146
Mayor, Margret 104
Mazyck, Paul 64
Mazycke, Danl 22
Meetze, George 11
Meetze, John 9, 13(2), 17, 90, 98, 130, 132(2), 134, 150
Mellard, James H. 100
Merit, Abraham 124
Metse, John 144
Mettze, Yost 128
Metz, Adam 66
Metz, David 14
Metz, George 14, 60, 148
Metz, Henry 66
Metz, J. Henry 66
Metz, Jacob 16
Metz, Jesse 148
Metz, John 5, 56, 84, 148
Metz, John Jr. 17

Metz, John Sr. 17
Metz, Joseph 15
Metz, Lewis 148
Metz, Nancy 16
Metz, Peter 15
Metz, Yost 60(2), 142
Metze, Daniel 146
Metze, Henry 150
Metze, Lewis 144
Meze, Daniel 8
Mickler, Andrew 108
Mickler, Christian 142(2), 148
Mickler, Jacob 108
Mickler, Peter 108
Milar, Henry 102
Millard, James H. 62(2)
Miller 142
Miller, Henry 4, 88, 102, 120(2)
Miller, John 56, 84, 150
Miller, Peter 32
Milton, William H. 142
Minick, G. B. 32, 36, 40
Minick, George 92(2)
Minick, George B. 2, 32, 34
Minick, Henry F. 14
Minick, Jacob 14, 144
Minick, John 40, 66, 92
Minick, John Junr 6
Minick, John Senr 92
Minick, Mary 8
Minick, Wm 2, 32(2), 36
Mitchel, Forest 13
Mitchel, Sion 13
Mitchel, Wm. C. 12
Montz, George 72, 140
Morgan, Daniel 14
Morgan, Spence 48
Morgan, Spencer 74(4)
Morris, Samuel 138
Moutz, George 44
Muller, H. 5
Muller, Henry 9, 48, 54, 76, 82(3), 90, 102, 106, 126(2), 128, 144
Murph, John 108
Murphy, John D. A. 142, 146

Nees, Jacob 34
Neese, Henry 130, 132
Neese, Jacob 144
Nicholas, Jacob 8
Nicholas, John 50
Nicholas, John Senr 56
Nicholas, Mary 8, 90, 124
Nichols, John 4
Nonemaker, Jacob 50
Nounemaker, Jacob 62(2), 76
N. C., B. County 120
Norts(?), Zachariah 44
Norts, Zacharias 72

Oswalt, Catharine 4, 78
Oswalt, Elizabeth 104, 116, 140, 146
Oswalt, George 9, 52, 80, 116(2)
Oswalt, George Junr 80
Oswalt, Godfrey 110
Oswalt, H. 112
Oswalt, Henry 5, 9, 80(2), 120(2), 142, 146
Oswalt, Henry & wife 40, 52
Oswalt, Jacob 116
Oswalt, John 48, 76, 150
Oswalt, John Junr 32

Oswalt, Levy 66
Oswalt, Mathias 40, 44, 72, 132(2)
Oswalt, Michael 4, 32, 98(2), 108(2), 112, 120
Oswalt, Michael Jr. 106
Oswalt, Samuel 24, 50, 76, 98(2), 138, 140
Oswalt, Susan 112
Oxner, Elizabeth 144

Page, Benjamin 126
Paker, Lewis 90
Passinger, Elizabeth 134(2)
Patrick 126
Patrick, Christian 70
Patton, James & Co 34
Patton, John 114(2), 118, 128, 130, 142
Patton, Messrs 34(2)
Pearce, R. 4
Pearson, John 144
Pellam, Charles 62
Pence, Rosana 28
Pepper, John 130
Perey, Nancy 44
Perey, William 44
Permenter, Evan 148
Perry, Sion 128
Peterbough, Michael 46
Pickey, Uriah 17
Pickley, Jacob 10, 13
Pickly, Joseph 11
Pickley, Samuel 10
Pinckney, Charles 68
Pinckney, Lueisa 60
Plimail, Michael 60
Plymail, Susannah 142
Poindexter, Sarah 142
Poindexter, Thomas K. 4, 14(2), 20, 36, 48, 76(2), 130, 142, 146
Polock, Frances 108
Pool 142
Pool, H. S. 118
Pool, William 122(2)
Pou, James 18, 22, 46, 52, 66, 72
Pou, James (Sheriff) 38(2)
Pou, Lewis 10, 11, 46, 72
Pound, Daniel 28
Pous, James 5
Price, George 112, 128, 140(2)
Price, George Junr 140
Price, George Snr 140

Quattlebom, John 4, 64, 68(2), 92, 120
Quattlebom, Mathias 20, 38, 68, 96
Quiter, Thomas 8

Radcliff, Richard 82
Ragin, D. 108
Ragnous, John 28
Raimick, Peter 28
Rall, Catharine 94, 132(2)
Rall, Christian 13, 15, 106
Rall, Daniel 142(3)
Rall, Fredk 13, 15, 24
Rall, George 68, 94, 120, 128(2), 140, 142(2)
Rall, Jacob 12, 15, 46, 54, 72, 82, 96, 106, 126(3), 140, 142
Rall, Jacob Jr. 134
Rall, John 14, 150
Rall, Nancy 106

Rall, Thos 15(2), 26, 66(2)
Rambo, Daniel 4, 34, 76, 100, 134
Rambo, Laurence 4, 100
Rambo, Saml 34
Ramsay, John 130
Rankin, John Jur. 88
Rankin, John Senr 88
Rankins, James 88
Rankins, John Senr 88
Ratcliff, Richard 54
Ravenell, Daniel 64
Rawl, Wm. L. 144
Rea, Maria 4
Redman, Jane 100
Redman, Peter 100, 28, 48, 56, 84, 92, 96
Redmond, John 42
Redman, Simon 50, 76
Rekert, George 140
Rekert, Madalene 140
Rhaw, Jesse W. 5
Rhay, Jesse W. 28, 56
Rice, Jacob 11, 14, 50(2), 78(3), 142
Rice, John 16
Richardson, Anna 32
Richardson, David 138
Richardson , James 104
Richardson,Levi 104
Richardson, Samuel 94
Richardson, Solomon 104
Richardson, Rhoda 104
Rickert, John 66
Riddle, Honorious 66, 98, 108
Ridlehoober, George 140
Riser, George 128, 140, 142
Rish, Adam 150
Rish, Elizabeth 32
Rish, John 150
Rish, Rosana B. 34
Risinger, David 13, 40
Risinger, Jacob 100
Rister, Christian 4, 28, 60
Rister, David 34
Rister, Frederick 34(2)
Rister, J. A. 13
Rister, John A. 9
Rister, John Adam 4, 60
Rister, John Jacob 34
Rives, Hanah 60
Rives, James 4
Rives, Simon and others 60
Rives, Thomas 8, 9, 88
Roberts, Absalom 12, 15, 90
Roberts, Asel 12, 90(2), 102
Rodd, Eliz. 104
Roden, Catharine 140
Roden, George 140
Rodwitz(?), John 9
Roffman, Christopher 144
Rogers, Elizh 32
Rogers, James 10, 44, 72
Roof, Benjamin 76, 150, 48, 62
Roof, Godfrey 48(2), 62, 76(2)
Roof, Henry 104(2), 132
Roof, John 48, 76, 104, 150
Roof, Reuben 146
Rooks, John 56, 84
Rouch, Jacob 22
Rouch, Michael 22, 60
Rudolph 134
Ruff, Henry 6, 18, 40, 64(2), 70, 118, 144
Ruff, John 15

Ruffs 132
Rumph, Jacob 98
Russell, Daniel S. 130, 134, 138
Rutledge, 148
Rutledge, H. M. 36
Rutledge, Henry M. 22(2), 24, 32, 46, 74, 112
Rutledge, Hon. Jno. 148
Ryner a free Negro 60

Saigoirth, John 22
St. John, Audeon 20, 22
St. Pauls Church 140
St. Peters Church 66
Saltzer, Adam 24
Saltzer, Mary 24
Sandford, Abraham 50
Satzer, Christopher 98
Sanford, William 50
Saunders, Frances 20
Saveur(?), John Mathias 54
Sawyer, Ansel 50, 78
Sawyer, Drury 52, 80, 90, 94(2), 100, 102, 134
Sawyer, George 12. 94
Sawyer, John 12, 64
Sawyer, John Senr 28, 92
Sawyer, Simpson 50, 78
Say, Esaias & wife 40
Sayler, Esayas 82
Saylor, E. & wife 34
Saylor, Esaias 82
Saylor, Esaias & wife 34
Saylor, Jacob 34
Schlice, Regann 72
Schlis, Regina 44
Schmitz, Adam 16, 142
Schmitz, H. F. Doctor 16
Schmitz, Maria 16
Scofield, William 60, 64
Scott, G. 94
Seagrest, Henry 28
Seas, Fredk 12
Seas, Mark 12
Seawright, Robert 66
Seay, John W. 14
Sebles, Henry 144(2)
See, Charles 22
See, George 22, 46
See, Henry 44, 46, 72, 74, 98
See, John 14, 24, 44, 46, 72, 116
See, Michael 26   Jesse 124
See, Nicholas 50, 66(6)
See, Sally 46
See, Susanah 44, 66, 72
See, William 11, 12, 42, 114, 142, 126
Segrest, Jacob 26, 38
Seibles, Henry 46, 56, 66, 84(3), 94, 118
Seibles, Henry Esqr 56
Seibles, Henry (Sheriff) 24, 28
Seibles, James 122
Seibles, John T. 54, 82, 102, 118, 128
Seibles, Sarah 60, 66, 118
Seibles, William 54, 82, 118
Seigels, Henry 72
Sely(?), John 32
Senn, David 32, 98
Senn, Elizh. 32
Senn, Henry 138
Senn, Jacob 146

Senn, John N. 84(2)
Senn, Matthias 7, 94, 128
Senn, William 94, 98, 126
Senterfit, Elizabeth 132
Senterfit, Henry 128
Senterfit, Stephen 132
Setzler, Adam 8
Setzler, George 4, 40, 70, 146
Setzler, John 4, 8, 146
Shaffer, Frederick 138, 98
Sharp, Christian 46
Sharp, Christopher 42, 74, 148
Sharp, J. 125
Sharp, J. Christopher 22
Sharp, John C. 26, 32, 56, 60, 62, 84(2), 108, 126, 142, 148(3)
Sharp, John C. Senr 118
Sharp, John D. 15, 38, 60, 62, 66, 142(2)
Sharp, John David 32(2)
Sharp, Mary 138
Sharp, Michael 34, 62
Sharp, Michael J. 38
Shaver, John Fredrick 36
Shealey, John W. Senr 76
Sheally, David 148
Sheally, John 92
Shealy, John Senr 148
Sheally, John W. 116
Shealy, Andrew 20
Shealy, Andrew W. 96
Shealy, A. W. 12
Shealy, Christena 26
Shealy, John 9
Shealy, John Jun. 146
Shealy, John Senr 146
Shealy, John Windle 20
Shealy, William Andrew 76
Sheely, John W. 68
Shelly, Andrew 116
Shely, John 36
Sheppard, Thomas 6
Shepperd, Thomas 110(2)
Sherb, Christopher 22(2)
Shirey, George 12
Shots, David 116(2)
Shotts, David 60
Shotts, Daniel 60
Shroder, Magdalena 138
Shrum, George B. 24
Shrum, George Barnard 66
Shrum, Prosey 66
Shular, Ann 28
Shular, John 7
Shular, Nicholas 24
Shular, Thomas 6
Shuler, John 8, 9, 98, 124
Shuler, Thomas 8, 98, 120, 124(3)
Shull, Daniel 18
Shull, Henry 18.
Shultz, John 18, 20, 40, 62
Shumperd, Peter 32   see also Chumperd
Shumpert, John 148
Shurs, John Westley 92
Siebles, Henry 2
Siebles, Jacob 2
Siebles, Sarah 2
Simmerly, John 84
Simons, Ann 40
Simons, Eliza 40
Simons, Rebeckah 40
Simons, Saul 126, 136

Simons, Wm. M. 40
Singly, F. 132
Singly, Margaret 104
Slagle, Jacob 18
Slagle, Wm. 5
Slappy, George 16, 28(2), 34(4), 78, 148
Slappy, Jac C. 148(2)
Slappy, Jacob C. 16, 28, 78
Slappy, John 28
Slappy, Margaret 14, 26, 70
Slappy, Reuben H. 10
Slappy, Reuben Hayley 40
Slappy, Reubin 148
Slappy, Several 150
Slappy, Uriah 40
Sleigel, William 18
Slice, Conrod 16, 124
Slice, Elias 150
Slice, Rachel 148
Slice, Uriah 16
Sligh, Solomon 104
Smith 132
Smith, B. 58
Smith, Catharine 2
Smith, Daniel 126, 144
Smith, Eleanor 16
Smith, Geo. L. 132
Smith, James 10
Smith, James Y. 16
Smith, John 22, 54, 82
Smith, Luther 132
Smith, Rachel 142
Smith, Samuel 127
Smith, Stephen 90
Smith, Thomas 2
Smoke, Jacob 60
Smoke, Michael 60
Snelgrove, Abner 34(2), 132, 134
Snelgrove, Baruch 2, 11
Snelgrove, Carey 140
Snelgrove, John 24(2), 34(3), 44, 72, 82, 126, 140
Snelgrove, John Junr 24
Snelgrove, John Senr 54
Snelgrove, William 4, 20(2), 34(3), 52(2), 64, 78, 80, 132, 134
Snelgrove, Wm (Sheriff) 40
Snider, George 50, 96, 124
Snider, Jacob 46, 50, 72, 78
Snider, John 50(3), 66, 76, 78(3), 116(2)
Snider, Mathias 50(2), 76, 78(2)
Snider, Sibbelly 10
Snider, Sophia 50
Snider, Susanna 48, 76, 50
Son, Agnes 14
Son, Andrew 10, 14, 140, 142
Sonn, Mary Agnes 10
Souter 54
Souter, Gasper 6, 46(2), 54(3), 74(4), 80(3), 82
Souter, Jacob 6, 54, 56, 80, 84(2), 94, 124
Souter, John 6, 46(3), 54(2), 74(4), 82(2)
Souter, Joseph 46
Sox, Godlep 138, 94
Spears, Charles 130
Spears, John 92
Spence, Robert 120
Spignar, George 88
Spires, Sarah 142
Spraggins, Thomas 140
Stack, Abram 40

Stack, Jacob 40
Stack, John 60, 148
Stack, Lewis 40, 132
Stack, Michael 64
Stagner, William 16
Stark, A. B. 118
Stark, Alexr B. 14, 22(5), 26(2), 28
Stark, Henry R. 146
Stark, Robert 38
Stark, Sarah 14
Stedham, George & wife 38
Stephens, J. W. 148
Stewart, Alexander 17, 138, 150
Stidham, George 28, 106
Stillman, Allen C. 140
Stingley, George 12, 15
Stingley, Godfrey 13, 14
Stingeley, Jacob 14, 138
Stingely, John 12
Stingley, Sarah 12
Stock, Christena 64
Stock, Michael 60, 64
Stone, Ester 38
Stone, Seth 38
Stotes, David 46
Stoudemeyer, Geo. 40(2)
Strother, George J. 40
Strother, Joseph 114
Strother, Mary 40
Strupe, Jacob 54
Stuck, Michael 9
Sturkie, Benjamin 100
Sullan, Harmon 8
Summer, George 24(2)
Summer, Henry 6, 20(2)
Summer, John 6, 56(2), 84
Summer, Mary 6
Summer, Nicholas 24
Summer, Wm 2, 6, 12, 138
Summers, William 104
Surgener, Elizabeth 108, 140
Swaigard, John 32
Sweatenburg, Wm. Junr 150
Swecard, John 74
Sweetenberg, F. 134
Sweetenberg, Wm. 130
Sweetonberg, Wm. 24
Swettenburg, Frederick 112
Swicard, Joh. 144
Swicard, John 46
Swicard, John J. 64
Swigart, Christian 50, 78
Swigtenburg, Eberhard 38
Swinney, John 104
Swygerts 134
Swygert, Christian 11(2), 88
Swygert, George 24(2), 88, 146
Swygert, J. J. 16
Swygert, Jacob 14, 146
Swygert, John 10, 138
Swygert, John Jun. 138
Symons, Elizabeth 62
Symonds, William M. 62

Tarer, Andrew 144(2)
Tarer, Christener 144
Tarer, Mary M. 144
Taree, Susan 144
Tarer, Susannah 138
Tarrar, Andrew 46
Tarrer, Andrew 74, 60

Taylor 104
Taylor, Adam 116, 144
Taylor, Celia 104
Taylor, Elizabeth 104, 132
Taylor, George 12, 144, 146
Taylor, Henry 130
Taylor, Henry Senr 90
Taylor, Henry P. 114
Taylor, Jacob 44, 72
Taylor, James H. 68, 128
Taylor, John 12, 36, 38, 88, 90, 114,
              116, 128, 130, 144
Taylor, Jonathan 106, 142, 144, 150
Taylor, Lavinia 13
Taylor, M. C. 32
Taylor, Michael 116, 150
Taylor, Ruth 104, 110, 124
Taylor, Sarah 98, 104
Taylor, Simon 22
Taylor, Thomas Senr 114(2)
Taylor, William 12, 15, 104, 114, 130,
               132, 148, 150
Taylor, William P. 12
Thomas, John 5, 7, 9, 10
Threat, John 92
Threewits, John 66
Threewitts, L. W. 36(2)
Threwits, Lew Ellen 10
Timmerly, Eve Margaret 50
Timmerly, Margaret 50
Touber, Philip & wife 64
Turner, James 38
Turner, Thomas 38
Turnipseed, A. M. S. 108
Turnipseed, John B. 108
Turnipseed, Jacob 50, 78(2)
Turnipseed, Jacob Junr 50
Tutt, Richard 42
Tutt, Gabriel H. 42(2)
Tyler, Jacob 36, 38, 124
Tyler, John 56, 84

Unger, Mary 14, 12
Unger, Zachariah 12, 14, 130

Vanderhorst 110
Vansant, Jacob 150
Vansant, John W. 44, 72
Vanzant, Nicholas 40, 102
Vanzant, Shadrack 150
Vick, Alexr 134
Vick, Brinkly 8, 142(2)
Vick, Mary 8

Wacter, Adam 130
Walker, Daniel 18
Walker, Jeremiah 56, 84
Walker, Samuel 68, 122
Waring, R. H. 112
Warne, Jacob 20
Warren, Thomas 114
Warren, Thomas Senr 108
Warring, Robert 15
Waters, Richard 104
Waters, Sion 100(2), 138
Watkins, Zedekiah 108
Watson, Elijah 15
Watt, James 54, 82
Watt, John 54(2), 82(2)
Watters, Philemon Esqr 122
Watters, Wilkes B. 120

Waver, David Senr 116
Wearts, John Henry 98
Weaver, David 26(2), 102, 134, 148
Weaver, George 120
Weaver, H. 110
Weaver, Henry 48, 56, 74, 84, 104, 108(2),
              112, 120(5)
Weaver, Henry Junr 120
Weaver, Samuel 94, 112(2)
Wecker, Mathias 26
Weed, John 5, 124, 138
Weightenburg, Fredrick 38
Wellesson, Thos T. 92
Wessinger, Jacob Junr 114
Wessinger, John 86, 126
Wessinger, John & wife 56
Wessinger, Mathias 56, 86
Wessinger, Michael 14, 138
Wessinger, Samuel Junr 7
Wessinger, Susana 86, 56
Wessinger, Ulrick 38(2)
Wessinger, Uriah 6
Whray, Jesse W. 84
Wicker, Mathias 48, 76 see also Wecker
Wiggers, Christopher 138
Wiggers, Christopher H. 68
Wilds, Thos 146
Wiles, Thomas 142
William, Abner 84
William, Joel 80, 84
Williams, Abner 20, 56, 80
Williams, Agner 52
Williams, David 40
Williams, Henry 114
Williams, Joel 52, 56, 134
Williams, John 62
Williams, Joseph 32, 36, 52, 80
Williams, Levi 42
Williams, Richard 36
Williams, Rignal 148(2)
Williams, Saml 94
Williams, Stephen 44, 72, 94, 150
Williamson, Charles 48
Willisson, Thos T. 100, 118(2), 122, 144
Willison, Thos J. Esqr 94
Willisson, Thos T. Esqr 94, 114
Wilson, John 40
Wilson, Mary 148
Wilson, Theophilus 54, 82
Wilson, William 102, 98
Wing, Bersheba 124
Wing, John 18, 104, 124
Wing, Mary 64
Wing, Nancy 124
Wing, Polly 124
Winkhouse, Catharine Elizabeth 8
Winkhouse, Revd. Jno. H. 8
Wingard, Benjamin 68
Wingard, Christian 98, 106
Wingard, Daniel 42, 70
Wingard, George 22, 134
Wingard, Henry 20(2)
Wingard, Jeremiah 146(2)
Wingard, Joshua 98
Wingard, Mary 126
Wingard, Michael 48(2), 76(2), 98(2)
Wingard, Saml 22, 60, 70, 90(2), 98
Wingard, Sarah 126
Wingard, Thomas 116
Wingard, William 22, 70, 100, 106
Wingart, George 60

Wingart, Samuel 60
Wingart, Samuel Jur. 60
Wingert, Mathias 8   Winkhouse, Jno H. & catherine Elizabeth 8
Wise, Anna 124
Wise, Frederick 4, 36
Wise, George 20, 28, 36, 108
Wise, Mary 4
Wise, Michael 38, 68, 114
Wise, Michael Junr 44
Wissenhunt, Peter 6
Wissenhunt, William 6
Withers, John 13, 104
Witt, Martin 114, 132
Wolfe, Jacob 10, 144
Wolf, John 56, 144
Wolfe, John 10, 60, 70, 84
Wolf, Joseph A. 144
Wood, John 92(2)
Woolley, Miner 108(4)

Yonce, Mathias 68
Young, Levi 94
Younginger 134
Younginger, George 50, 114
Younginger, John 100
Younginer, Margaret 50, 78, 108
Younginger, Sebastian 8, 50(2), 52, 78(3),
                      92
Zeigler, Adam 144
Zigler, Adam 142
Zimmerly, Margaret 4, 78

Heritage Books by Brent H. Holcomb:

Bute County, North Carolina Land Grant Plats and Land Entries

*CD: Early Records of Fishing Creek Presbyterian Church,
Chester County, South Carolina, 1799–1859*

CD: Kershaw County, South Carolina Minutes of the County Court, 1791–1799

CD: Marriage and Death Notices from The Charleston [S.C.] Observer, *1827–1845*

CD: South Carolina, Volume 1

*CD: Winton (Barnwell) County, South Carolina Minutes of
County Court and Will Book 1, 1785–1791*

*Early Records of Fishing Creek Presbyterian Church, Chester County,
South Carolina, 1799–1859, with Appendices of the Visitation List of
Rev. John Simpson, 1774–1776 and the Cemetery Roster, 1762–1979*
Brent H. Holcomb and Elmer O. Parker

Kershaw County, South Carolina Minutes of the County Court, 1791–1799

*Marriage and Death Notices from Columbia, South Carolina Newspapers, 1838–1860;
Including Legal Notices from Burnt Counties*

Marriage and Death Notices from The Charleston Observer, *1827–1845*

Memorialized Records of Lexington District, South Carolina, 1814–1825

*Winton (Barnwell) County, South Carolina Minutes of
County Court and Will Book 1, 1785–1791*

South Carolina Deed Abstracts, 1773–1778, Books F-4 through X-4

South Carolina Deed Abstracts, 1776–1783, Books Y-4 through H-5

South Carolina Deed Abstracts, 1783–1788, Books I-5 through Z-5

York County, South Carolina Will Abstracts, 1787–1862 [1770–1862]

www.ingramcontent.com/pod-product-compliance
Lightning Source LLC
Chambersburg PA
CBHW062003180426
43198CB00036B/2170